Learn to
CROSS-COUNTRY SKI
in One Day

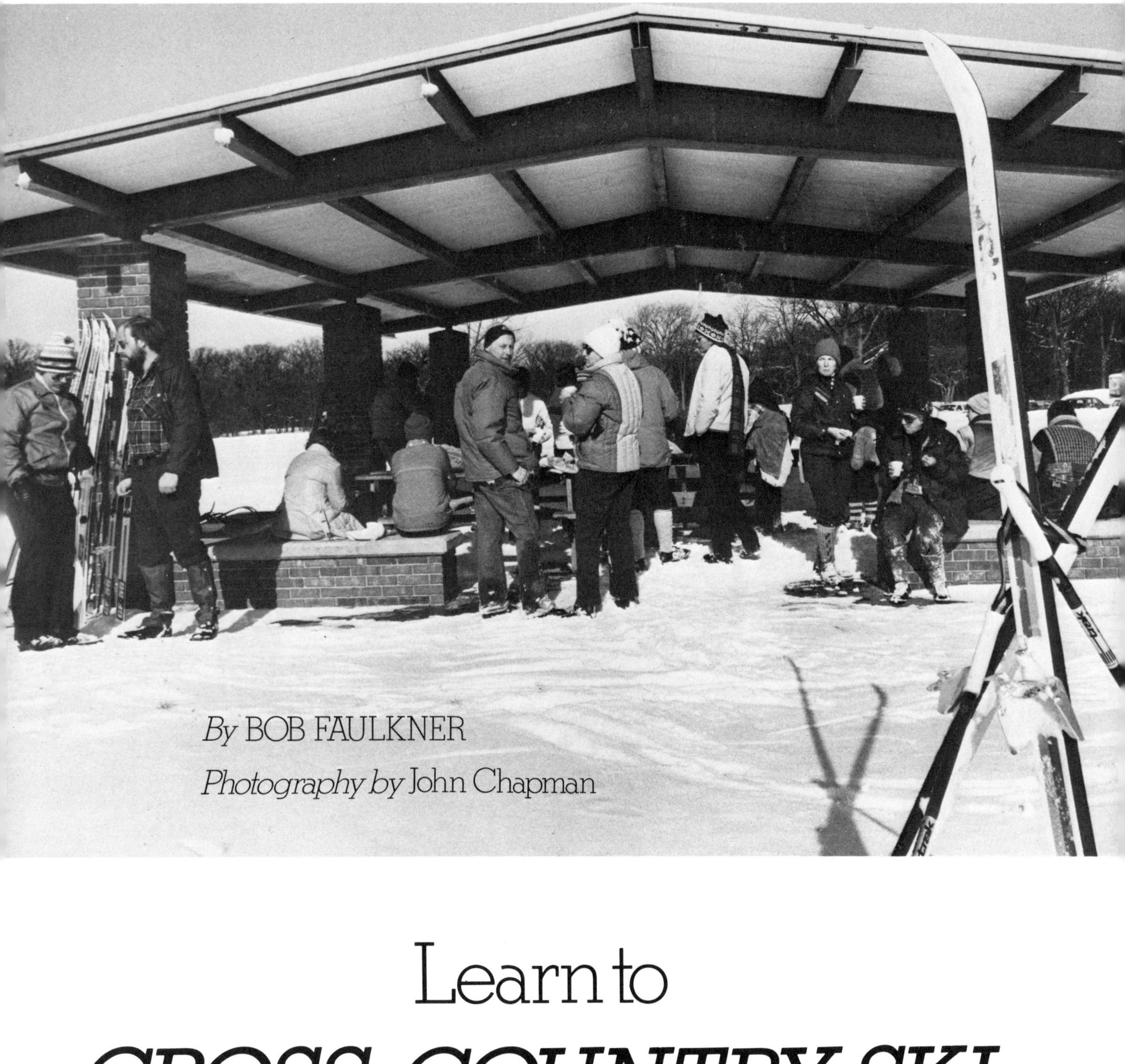

By BOB FAULKNER

Photography by John Chapman

Learn to
CROSS-COUNTRY SKI
in One Day

RAND McNALLY & COMPANY
Chicago / New York / San Francisco

This book is dedicated to John Lindstrom, whose enthusiastic lecture and demonstration fanned the spark that became my enthusiasm; to Lee Smith, whose hurled challenge made me mad enough to get up out of my chair and develop the course; and to my thousands of students . . . who have taught me to ski!

John Lindstrom

Photographs on pages 1, 2, 3, and 6 courtesy of The SUN Newspapers, LaGrange, Illinois.

Copyright © 1978 by RAND McNALLY & COMPANY
All rights reserved
Printed in the United States of America
by RAND McNALLY & COMPANY
Library of Congress Catalog Card Number: 78-7097
First Printing, 1978

FOREWORD

Imagine yourself walking barefoot down a dusty, tree-lined country road on a sunny afternoon in early summer. Gentle breeze, birds singing, plenty of time to get where you are going and nothing particular to do when you get there. Your feet move automatically, and you haven't a care about staying warm and dry. You have the rest of your life to be in a hurry; today it is just stroll and relax.

Do you know that feeling? that glow? You could make a million dollars if you could bottle it. Well, some of us know how to generate that same sense of well-being in the middle of winter!

That's the way millions of us cross-country skiers feel. We are torn between letting you in on it and keeping it "our little secret."

Take this course and see.

CONTENTS

✳

Introduction · 8

Hour 1. YOUR INDOOR ORIENTATION · 13

Hour 2. DOING IT OUTSIDE · 37

Hour 3. SLOWING DOWN & STOPPING · 57

Hours 4. & 5. DOWNHILL TURNS
         & SIX WAYS UPHILL · 69

Hour 6. HOW TO CROSS-COUNTRY SKI · 91

Hour 7. "BIG KID STUFF" · 103

Afterword · 123

✳

INTRODUCTION

HI. I'M BOB FAULKNER; I'M YOUR SKI INSTRUCTOR. I SKI FOR FUN, AND I'M GOING TO TEACH YOU TO DO THE SAME. I'M GOING TO TAKE YOU, STEP BY STEP, THROUGH THE SAME COURSE AND THE SAME EXERCISES YOU WOULD GO THROUGH IF YOU HAD SIGNED UP FOR MY SCHOOL AND HAD SHOWN UP, PROPERLY DRESSED WITH YOUR SHINY NEW EQUIPMENT, AT 10:30 ONE BRIGHT WINTER MORNING AT OUR HILLY, FOREST "CAMPUS."

I'm going to take the same attitude toward you that I take with *everybody* in my ski classes: I will assume that you are a complete novice, a first-timer who never had a pair of cross-country skis on before. It's a good assumption to make even if you have several years of skiing behind you, Alpine or Nordic. If you've skied some, you'll probably have a little easier time with your snowplow, your downhill, and that sort of thing.

You can do these "hours" all at once or in little "bites." I recommend you do them all in one day, as we do at the school. Most of the language in the book is exactly the same as that used at the school, where I conduct one of the most successful cross-country ski courses in the Midwest, a high-intensity, six-hour, one-session experience. But, you ask, is it *really* possible to learn to cross-country ski in just six hours?

Most emphatically, *YES!*

Cross-country is a very simple sport to learn, and it is one of the *safest* things you can do . . . if you prepare yourself, have good equipment, and take the few simple precautions that I'll cover as we go along.

Yes, you *are* going to be a trifle stiff tomorrow, but not bad. A few "new" muscles will be sore, but nothing debilitating! You *will* be tired tonight (hope you didn't have a dinner party planned). You'll sleep like a log, as much from all the fresh air as from the exercise, and you will feel tremendous!

Let's define a term here, first. This activity is popularly known as "cross-country." That conjures up memories to me of high school distance runners plunging ahead mile after mile, "pick 'em up and lay 'em down." Lots of work and (presumably) very little enjoyment; it wasn't done for joy!

Perhaps that is still one popular interpretation of cross-country skiing: plodding through the snow mile after mile. I know that's what most "downhillers"* think: "That's a lotta work . . . me, I like to *ski,* you know, going fast downhill."

Well, students, so do I. Only I "gave up" lift lines and crowds and tows and lifts of all kinds, as well as heavy, uncomfortable boots and all that clothing to keep me warm during the 45 or 50 minutes of every ski hour when I was *waiting* to ski. Now, when I ski for an hour, I get in an hour's skiing. I can do it two blocks from my suburban home, or I can drive to a different area for a change of scenery.

And I don't have to pay to ski unless I want to. Resorts are opening more groomed and marked trails every year, and for the most part they're great! On every trail you'll find some steep uphills and a wild downhill or two. *Not* boring!

Cross-country is Nordic skiing. Uphill, downhill, flatland, woods, stream crossings, birds, animal tracks (actual critters, too, if you're lucky), sun, moon, stars, *and* warmth and comfort out-of-doors!

If you think you're going to buy a cheap pair of boards and just go for a "walk" across a snow-covered golf course, you fail to understand what cross-country is all about. We're talking about skiing here. And skiing is *all the same,* Alpine and Nordic. Sure,

---

*Downhiller: An Alpine skier, one who must, because of rigid, inflexible equipment, be carried to the top of the ski hill by motor-driven lifts before he can descend, using gravity for propulsion.

there are differences, some of them big, but skiing is skiing and has been for 4,000 years! If you know somebody who just shuffles along on the flat and avoids hills because they're "too hard" to climb or "too dangerous" to go down, he needs our kind of help!

During the six hours of your one-day lesson, you're going to learn to ski. On cross-country skis! You'll be able to do at least five different turns, you'll know the difference between them, and you'll understand why we use different turns at different times. You'll be able to ski uphill, and you'll learn to ski on the flat, making better time and covering ground more easily than you could by any other means except snowmobile.

And here's a point of view I'll bet you've never considered: covering ground on cross-country skis in winter is much faster and more enjoyable than walking over the same uphill, down-dale, through-the-woods route in summer! On cross-country skis you're moving—you're not a pedestrian! That's what Nordic skiing is all about.

I've given this course to several hundred "Alpine-trained" skiers, and every one of them has said something like: "This is a blast! Why it's just like 'real' skiing. I thought it was going to be dull, and I thought it was going to be much harder work than it is." And even trained Alpine skiers learn more about skiing, including an "old-time" turn that you can't do on downhill skis—and, man, does it work!

What we're going to learn is how to do it all, the "easy way." Many of the turns are executed in exactly the same manner as with rigid Alpine equipment, but we will go back and analyze the turns and find out why they work. We have to because we can't force turns to the extent that they can be "muscled" with downhill gear. We'll have to think more, understand what we are doing better, and ski with more finesse in order to accomplish the same goals. It's kind of "back to basics."

You really should do your learning with a friend or a small group of friends. Cross-country skiing is much like Alpine skiing in that respect: it's a most convivial experience. Skiing produces much joy, and it is fun to share that joy with friends. Of course, you *can* learn alone.

This course is laid out in "hours." Take this book outside with you, or read each hour inside, and copy the timecheck list at the end for your on-the-snow "cheat sheet." It will go best if you master your skills one hour at a time, pausing to read the instructions before launching into the next hour. Practice each maneuver until you've mastered it. I've put more emphasis on those areas that have proven to be the "stickiest" at the ski school.

I hate to brag, but we're graduating 75 to 150 skiers each snowy weekend. The total now has reached several thousand. My reason for mentioning this is to emphasize one caution: *do the hours in the order in which they are presented*. There is a reason for this *exact* order, which has been revised and re-revised, then tried and proven week after week for four winters in a row.

Mostly, the hours cover practical, "how-to" things, and techniques are amply illustrated to clear up any questions. I've kept the text as brief as possible. I've tried to put as much skiing into as few words as I can so that it won't take you a day just to *read* a course that promises to teach you to cross-country ski in that amount of time. Why wade through pages of words that won't get you skiing any faster.

This is a participatory, action course, not a reader! You have to listen carefully first, and then go out and do it. So please don't speed read. Instead, when you read the "hour" indoors before you go outside, do it actively, standing, bending, and going through the motions.

A profound change is about to take place in your life! It will happen on both the physical and mental levels. Physically, you'll learn many new moves, gain confidence, and most likely develop a great deal of respect for a really fine winter outdoor activity. Mentally, you'll learn to love winter! That's one of the definitions of a skier. This course and cross-country skiing will positively and forever alter the way you think about snow and winter. You'll count the days till the first snow. You'll smell snow in the air and become just as enthusiastic as you were as a kid.

You'll probably watch less television, have fewer winter colds, lose some weight, feel a little better, have better skin color, and *maybe* even find that you're a bit more alert at work or in school.

Q. Who can learn from these lessons?
A. Anyone over the age of 8. This course is designed for adults, but nothing in the lessons is beyond the capabilities of the average 8- or 9-year-old. There is *no* upper age limit.

In my "live" course I've had students from 8 all the way up to 75. I've had only one failure, and to this day I can't understand why she (a normal, tennis-playing, married, early 30s mother of two) didn't catch on. She just couldn't do it. That's why you won't hear me say, "Anyone who can walk can cross-country ski."

I've taught the young, the old, the physically and mentally handicapped, the visually handicapped, and thousands of others. You are about to benefit from all of my words to all of those nice people.

The six hours contain all the techniques you will need for a *lifetime* of touring fun. But I've added a seventh hour . . . a sort of appendix that includes a few more skills, which go beyond the original intent of this book but are fun to know. In Hour 7 you'll find out about "helicopter" turns, the snowplow christie, parallel turns on skinny skis, and the famous telemark. You could *tour* forever and never need them, but, as you will hear me say more than once, going downhill is the most fun on *any* kind of skis. You should know, too, that advanced maneuvers can be done on your light, touring equipment.

Let me add one very realistic caution here. If you own this book for a whole winter and don't learn to ski, you might need the stimulus and discipline of an organized ski school. You *can* learn to ski from this volume but not if you just use it as decoration on your coffee table. You *can* take all winter if you wish, but it comes together so well in a single session that it is worth planning for, renting equipment in advance, and setting aside a day.

Now, let's get on about this business of learning a new "lifestyle."

Hour 1.

✳ SKIS

✳ BINDINGS

✳ BOOTS

✳ POLES

✳ DRESSING FOR THE WEATHER

✳ EXTRAS

✳ SURVIVAL

✳ FINDING YOUR PLACE TO LEARN

✳ CONDITIONING

Hour 1.

YOUR INDOOR ORIENTATION

HERE'S ALMOST EVERYTHING YOU'LL NEED TO KNOW ABOUT EQUIPMENT TO ENJOY YOUR LEARNING EXPERIENCE. WHAT YOU LEARN HERE AND WHAT YOU'LL LEARN DURING THE ACTUAL SKIING THAT FOLLOWS WILL GIVE YOU A PRETTY GOOD IDEA OF WHAT TO PURCHASE WHEN THE TIME COMES. A TYPICAL PACKAGE—SKIS, BOOTS, BINDINGS, AND POLES—COSTS BETWEEN $85 AND $150, DEPENDING ON QUALITY, TIME OF YEAR, AND SO FORTH. FIGURE ON SPENDING ABOUT $120, ALTHOUGH YOU CAN SAVE QUITE A FEW DOLLARS AT END-OF-SEASON SALES.

I'm not going to tell you *too* much about equipment, though, because it is changing and improving so rapidly that every month brings an innovation that makes something else obsolete. But that doesn't mean that your old "woodies" with 4-pin bindings (or even cables) are useless junk. That's not so. A friend and I have waxed up a pair of 75-year-old, 10-foot-long boards with leather straps and, by golly, they worked! At least they worked on the flat (uphill they were awful).

My best advice is to spend a couple of hours some Saturday morning visiting several nearby, involved ski shops, ones that have a large selection of cross-country equipment, ones with salespeople who ski, and, if possible, ones with instruction programs. They usually know more than the discount merchandisers and sports "department stores" that are jumping on the cross-country bandwagon.

Now let's learn a little about equipment: skis, bindings, boots, and poles. Let's get dressed correctly (I'm saving a little surprise about dressing until we get to that portion of the hour). I'll also share a few pre-lesson "survival" tips, things that will make the next six hours (and the rest of your *life*) safer and more enjoyable, and then help you pick a place where you can learn to ski.

SKIS. Worldwide cross-country popularity has caused a technological "explosion" in ski construction. You can still get "woodies," multi-lamination all-wood skis with hickory soles and "lignostone" edges, but all I can say is "you gotta wanna." Fiberglass, P-Tex, foam, and ABS are here! P-Tex 2000 is the best waxable base ever! No more need to pine-tar (though I'll miss the smell). No more worry about skiing on partially unprotected wooden soles, soaking up moisture. And wax really sticks to P-Tex; they're super easy to wax and maintain. And they're strong!

But waxing skis takes up *hours* of ski time . . . talking about waxing, thinking about waxing, *worrying* about waxing, putting on wax, changing wax, scraping off wax, figuring out what wax or combination of waxes is right . . . at this point in your learning, who cares? Rent and learn on good no-wax skis!

The school's motto is: "Learn to ski first; then learn to wax (if you want to)." "Waxless" skis have come of age and get better every year. Some of us "old timers" lament the passing of those beautiful all-wood, 47-lamination skis. But we realize that the new all-synthetic or synthetic/wood combination skis are stronger, lighter, and retain their camber better than any all-wood ski.

Fiberglass, foam, P-Tex, and ABS might not be as naturally beautiful, but they allow us to spend more time actually skiing—and that's what this sport is all about. It's cross-country *skiing* we all like, not cross-country ski *maintenance!*

By this time, it's no secret, I guess, that I'm a true convert: a former "wax head" who now believes wholeheartedly in fish scales for the recreational skier (and certainly for the beginner and student). So, by all means, take this course on good, waxless skis, and before you buy, rent several brands to try them out.

I'll admit to all purists that a perfectly waxed ski is better than any no-wax configuration I've ever tried. But no-wax skis

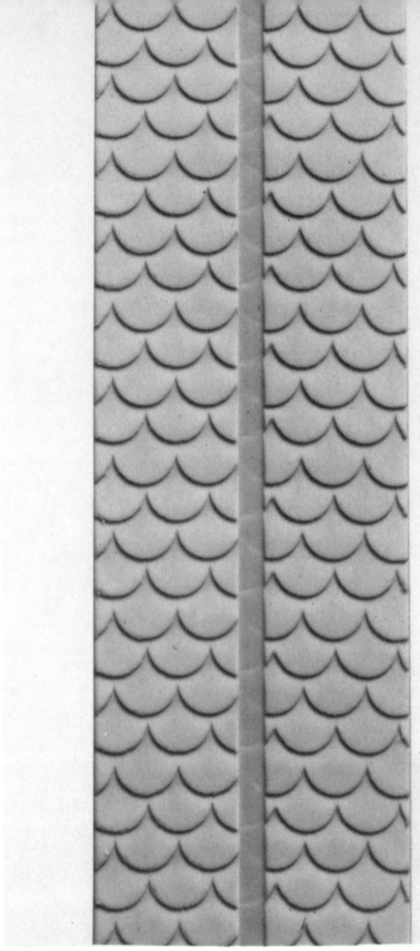

Top left. *Typical ski bottoms, left to right: stair-step, no-wax hickory/ "lignostone" edge; P-Tex 2000 (racing); fish-scale no-wax.* Top right. *Detail of fish scales.* Bottom. *Types of cross-country skis, left to right: racing; light touring/training; light touring; general touring.*

1.

work across a much wider range of snow conditions. Fish scales always work. And in certain instances, such as transitional snow and wet, slushy conditions, fish scales *can't be beat!*

In North America no-wax skis currently account for over 50 percent of sales, and they undoubtedly have contributed greatly to the rising popularity of cross-country skiing. This percentage figure will continue to go up every year! And here's a real shocker, purists: in Europe, the ancestral home of Nordic skiing, no-wax skis currently command almost 75 percent of sales!

One other very nice thing about the new wave of synthetic and mostly synthetic skis is that they are not nearly as subject to drying out in summer storage. You frequently can pick up some spectacular bargains in end-of-summer (pre-season) sales and do so with reasonable peace-of-mind if you buy a foam/fiberglass ski. Unfortunately for foes of planned obsolescence, "cosmetics" have taken hold of cross-country equipment, and people will know you've bought last year's skis! But at half-price . . . who cares!

Modern skis should hold their camber forever. Camber is the "arch" of the ski. My "originals," some nine winters old, lost most of their "bow" in the attic (the wrong place to store them) the first summer I had them and are now really "flat-footed." I still use them once in a while, and they work. But, frankly, it's just too darn much trouble to get them pine-tarred and waxed very often! I can ski three miles in the time it would take.

I do, incidentally, use several different "glide augmenters" on the fish-scale skis I wear when I instruct: a pressure spray, silver downhill on the tips and tail glide surfaces, and I've even run tips and tails through a hot waxer. You don't *need* to do any of this, but it does improve downhill and glide performance. Some racing skis currently use P-Tex 2000 gliding surfaces (for maximum waxability) and a fish-scale "kick area." You'll probably be able to buy this configuration in recreational skis in the next year or so.

A word of caution to end this discussion before we fit you out. Unlike buying a "racing bicycle" and riding it around for pleasure or using "racing skates" for pleasure skating because they're easy to handle, don't buy racing skis for recreational skiing! Here's why: recreational, light touring skis are available in a variety of stiffnesses (flex ranges). The "correct" light touring ski will have sufficient camber, or arch, to keep the kick portion off the snow when you are gliding. But the skis will be "soft" enough for you to get that kick patch down on the snow easily for power skiing and for climbing hills.

Light touring skis are typically 56 mm wide at the shovel, 50 mm at the waist, and 52 mm at the tail. This is called side cut (sometimes side camber), and it allows the ski to maneuver easily through all snow conditions from soft, unbroken snow to hard-packed, groomed tracks. It also makes the ski more turnable.

Bottom left. *Diagram of parts of a ski.* Bottom right. *Fitting cross-country skis by the old rule of thumb. The tip just touches the comfortably upraised wrist.*

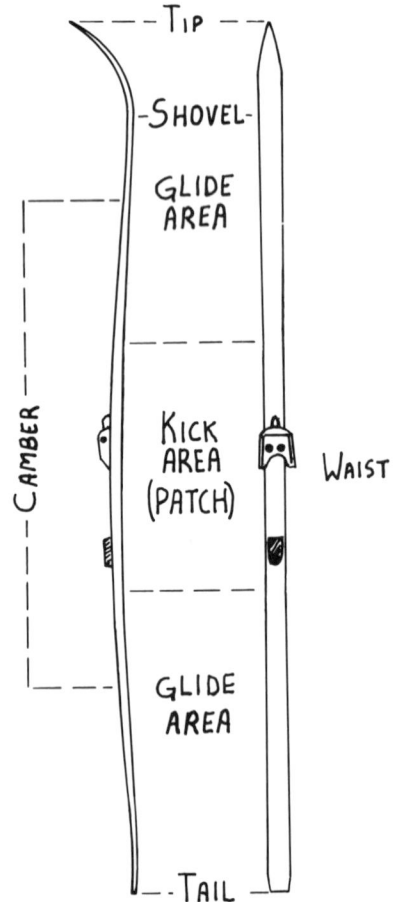

The racing ski, on the other hand, is typically very, very stiff through the center kick area. Many, in fact, have what is called "second camber," meaning that it is almost impossible for a beginning skier to get that kick portion into contact with the snow.

Racing skis require quite a different technique from that used by the touring skier. Racing skis also are narrower and straight cut—45 mm at the shovel, 45 mm at the waist, and 45 mm at the tail. Racing skis are lighter and much more fragile in the critical tip/shovel area. They are meant to be used only in prepared tracks. They are hard to turn, useless in deep, soft snow, and they cost a lot! Look at some (they're usually very pretty), and then buy light, touring skis.

What size skis should you use and how "stiff" should they be? Much depends on how good you are, how tall you are, and how much you weigh. For length, the old rule of thumb about reaching up comfortably above your head and having the ski tip touch your up-raised wrist is still as good as anything. Some of the new skis, stronger and more durable to the tenth power than the old all-wood skis of comparable cost, are *stiffer*, and that makes length not nearly as important as it once was. Skis 5 to 10 cm longer or shorter probably will be unnoticeable to the average skier. My 10-year-old son (a good skier) handles a pair of my sophisticated 210s with no difficulty, including kick turns, and my 5'5", 115-lb. wife once said, upon trying my new fiberglass/foam 210s: "I like my skis a little longer than this." The new, stiffer skis feel and handle like shorter models.

If you are exceptionally light for your height or heavier than "average" for your height, you'll want to consider a correspondingly longer or shorter ski. One of the jobs of a ski is to help distribute your weight evenly on the snow. Therefore, heavier usually equals longer; lighter equals shorter.

Here's the best way to judge the right length/stiffness combination for your height/weight. Stand on *both* skis on a hard, smooth floor. A crisp dollar bill should *just* slip underneath the skis at a point directly under your feet. If it slides through too

1.

Here's a chart that will give you a pretty good idea of the right ski length for your height and weight.

Children (under 125 lbs.)		Women			Men		
Height	Touring Ski Length	Height	Skiing Weight	Touring Ski Length	Height	Skiing Weight	Touring Ski Length
under 38"	150cm	5'0"–5'4"	100–115 115–130 125–140 135–150	185cm 190cm 195cm 195cm	5'4"–5'8"	125–147 145–170 155–185 175–225	195cm 200cm 205cm 210cm
38"–46"	150cm	5'3"–5'7"	100–115 115–130 125–140 135–150	190cm 190cm 195cm 200cm	5'7"–5'11"	125–147 145–170 155–185 175–225	200cm 205cm 210cm 210cm
48"–50" 52"–54"	150cm 160cm	5'6"–5'9"	100–115 115–130 125–140 135–150	190cm 195cm 195cm 200cm	5'10"–6'3"	125–147 145–170 155–185 175–225	205cm 210cm 215cm 215cm
4'8" 4'10"	170cm 170cm	5'8"–6'0"	100–115 115–130 125–140 135–150	195cm 200cm 200cm 205cm	6'0"–6'6"	125–147 145–170 155–185 175–225	210cm 215cm 215cm 215cm

Conversion Chart

Centimeters	Feet/Inches (approx.)
150	4'11"
160	5'3"
170	5'7"
175	5'9"
180	5'11"
185	6'1"
190	6'3"
195	6'5"
200	6'7"
205	6'9"
210	6'11"
215	7'1"
220	7'3"

easily, the skis are probably longer than you need, and if the dollar bill binds or won't go under the skis at all, obviously they're too short.

As I said earlier, if you are (or become) a very good skier, you'll want specific things in a ski, and by then you'll know how to select them and probably what brand and model you want. You undoubtedly will have a chance to try many different skis. Cross-country skiers like to trade equipment and "show off."

BINDINGS. Five or six years ago, all the countries and manufacturers agreed on a standard binding/boot sole configuration called the "Nordic Norm." It permits interchangeability between all boots and bindings, worldwide. As this is written, I advise you to stick with "Nordic Norm 75 mm" if they'll fit your size boots. The other sizes are "Norm 71 mm" for little feet and "Norm 79 mm" for you giants. Any brand of Nordic Norm bind-

Some typical bindings, front to back: metal with padded bale; Lexan semi-racing; metal with wire bale; cable type (child's).

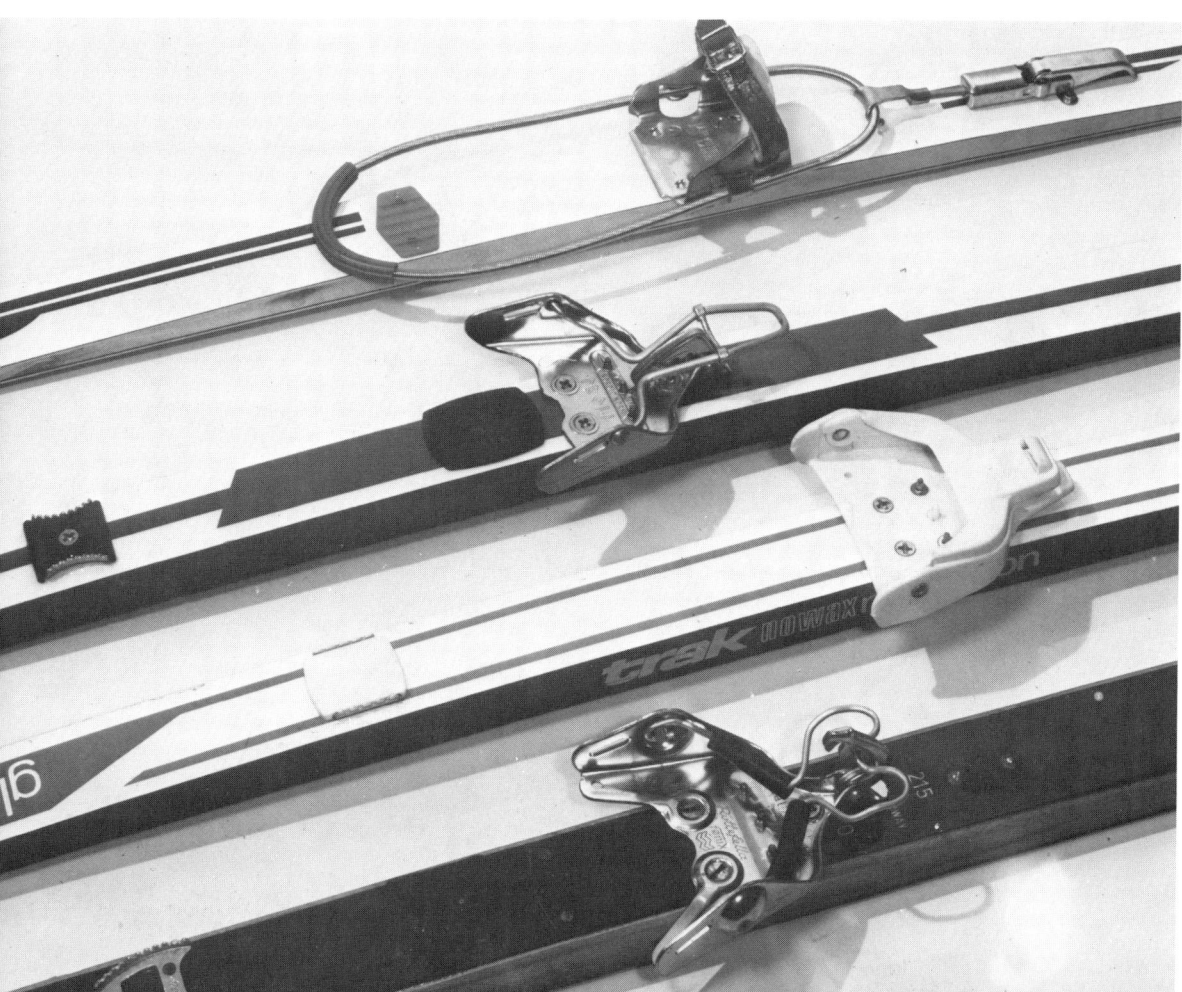

ings works fine. But check which one you think is the easiest to get on and off; they vary greatly in that respect.

Since Nordic Norm bindings fit 95 percent of all boots available worldwide, you can trade and compare skis with all your friends and you can usually rent skis that fit your boots. Some new bindings are nylon and are guaranteed for years. And they can be put on and removed in seconds. No more stooping or getting down on one knee.

Left. Boots and bindings. Left: Norm 50 "racing Norm" symmetrical binding. Right: typical Nordic Norm 75 mm with new nylon binding. Top right. One type of gaiter, or snow cuff. It keeps snow from caking around your ankle. Bottom right. A "high cut" boot with soft ankle padding. It provides some ankle support.

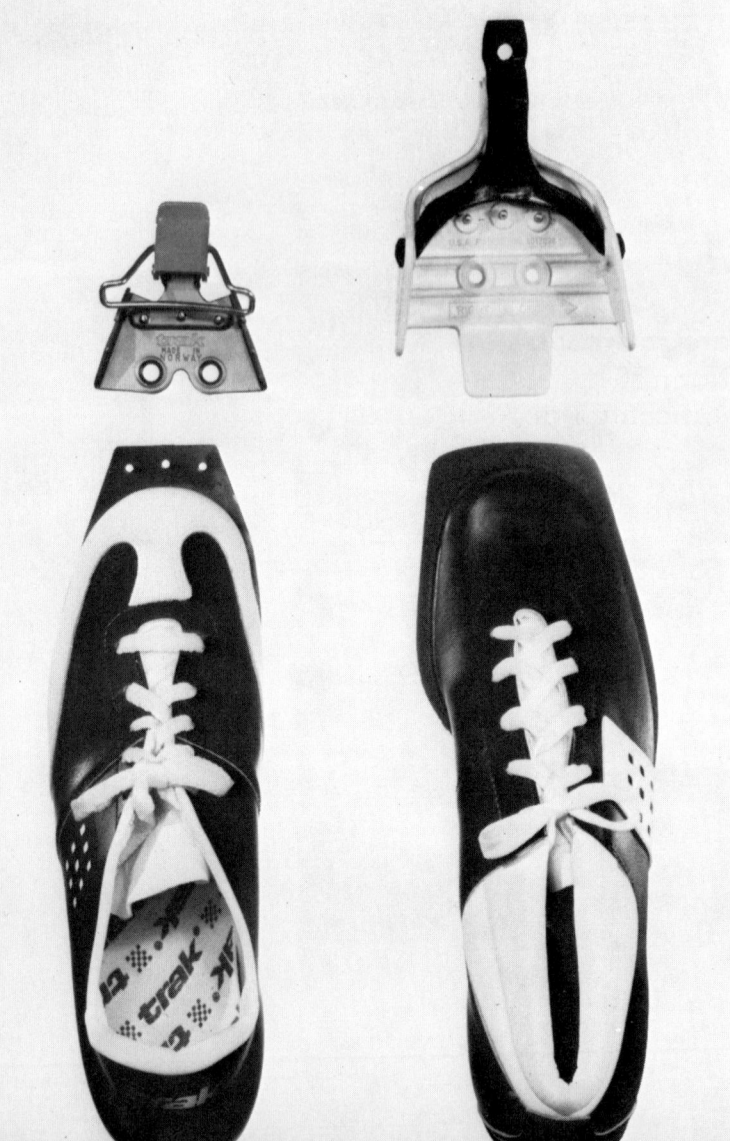
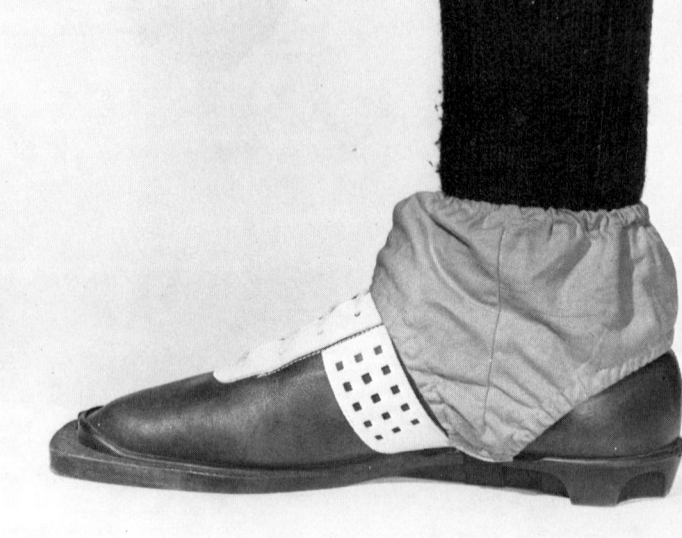

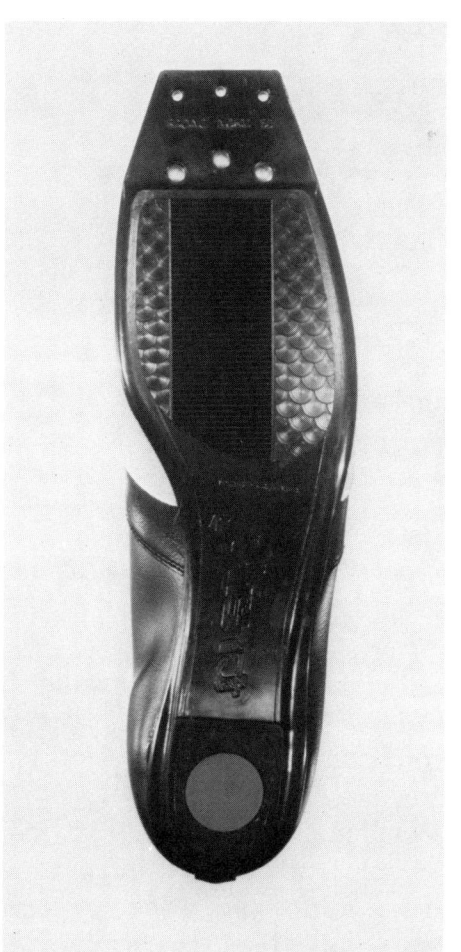 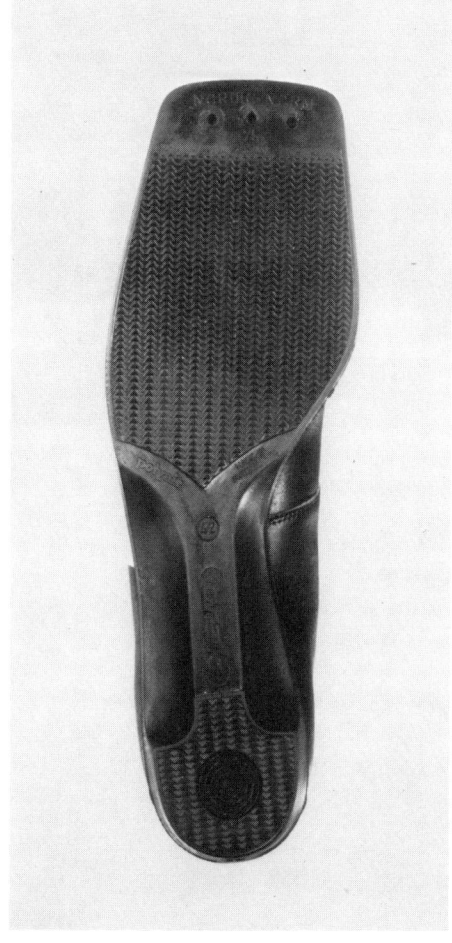

Left. *A typical Nordic Norm (75 mm) boot sole.* Right. *A Norm 50 sole. Note the soft rubber insert in heel for pin-type heel plate.*

Ask the shop where you trade about "Norm 50." They seem to be "coming fast," though they're still referred to as "racing Norm." Their advantages: skis are interchangeable (no more right or left) and boot soles in the Norm 50 configuration are more laterally stable, providing better ski control and easier forward foot flex while requiring less force for kick and glide.

BOOTS. Probably everyone is familiar with "ski boots." If you are a downhiller, you know they weigh "about 40 pounds apiece." They're inflexible, they make you walk around at a 20-degree angle, and if you *made* somebody wear them, they'd have you arrested for "cruel and unusual treatment." Of course, they're for a very limited and particular use: keeping wide, stiff skis under control while the skier is shooting down some mountain.

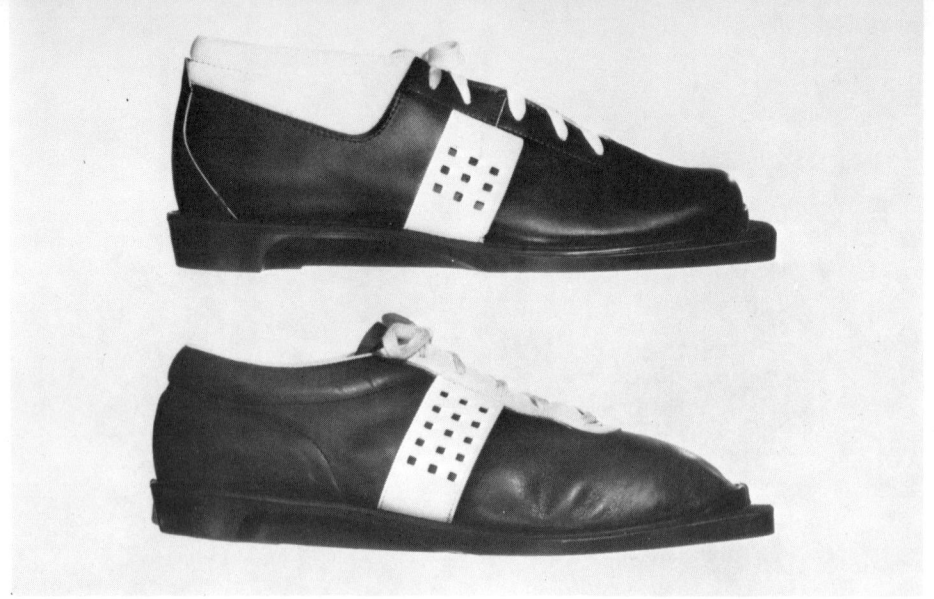

Two types of Nordic Norm "low cuts." Top boot has soft padded snow collar or "skree."

Cross-country ski boots are exactly opposite. They're light, flexible, and actually *comfortable*. You can walk around in them. You can dress at home and drive your car to where you intend to cross-country ski with your boots on!

Everybody has a pair of winter boots. They keep your feet warm and/or dry in all that cold, wet snow, so cross-country boots must be like galoshes? Well, just have a look at a rack of cross-country boots in your ski shop. They look like *shoes*. They're mostly low cut, like street shoes, and only one or two models have any lining. None of them are insulated or thick.

Q. How do your feet stay warm?
A. I'll bet I was asked that question about fifty dozen times, and I always attempted long, explanatory answers. Then it finally flashed on me—the answer that students would relate to. If your feet *did* get cold, then the racks would be full of big, fat, insulated rubber/nylon/foam snowmobile-type boots with funny long cross-country toes on them. You can't buy such boots because you don't need them. Your feet *aren't going to get cold*. I don't care if you say, "But my feet are cold from November first until the Fourth of July." They won't be when you're cross-country skiing because we know how to dress and dress correctly for each outing. You'll see why later on in this hour.

I prefer boots that are low cut, like street shoes or running shoes. Sometimes I wear gaiters (waterproof nylon leggings) to keep the snow from caking around my ankles, but even with low-cuts, I never get snow in my boots. (Never more than a few flakes anyway.) Unfortunately, I've never tried over-the-ankle boots, but everybody who has seems to like them a lot. Rent at least one pair of each before you decide to buy. Over-the-ankle boots do provide just a little more ankle support, but cross-country isn't much of an "ankle sport" anyway, so that's not too important unless you have terribly floppy ankles. (Do you fall off your shoes a lot?) Cross-country is mostly just like walking and not at all like ice skating, where you're trying to control a "knife blade on stilts."

Except for the new Norm 50 boots (which are all very low cut), everything that you can buy has the Nordic Norm (71, 75, and 79 mm) sole pattern and fits Nordic Norm bindings. In general, I like leather uppers, unlined. But some of the synthetic leather or nylon uppers are great, so it boils down to personal preference. All soles are now rubber composition or plastic, all are completely waterproof, and all are fused to the uppers so there's no way they can leak (even if that were a problem).

Here's a size conversion chart for boots, which mostly come in "European sizes" (metric). Be sure you are fitted, when you rent or buy, while wearing the socks you'll wear for skiing—two pairs.

CHILDREN		WOMEN		MEN	
Shoe Size	European Equivalent	Shoe Size	European Equivalent	Shoe Size	European Equivalent
9-10	28	5	35	5	37
11	29	6	36	5½	38
12	30	6½	37	6	39
13	31	7	38	7–7½	40
1	32	8	39	8–8½	41
2	33	9	40	9	42
3–3½	34	9½	41	9½	43
4	35	10	42	10–10½	44
4½	36			11	45
				12	46
				13	47
				13½	48

Top left. *How to fit your poles. The top of the handle should just touch the knob on the front of your shoulder when the tip is on a hard floor.* Top right. *Touring pole handles and straps. Left to right: fiberglass pole, plastic grip, nylon strap; Tonkin pole, cork grip, leather strap; Tonkin pole, plastic grip, leather strap; Tonkin pole, plastic grip, nylon strap; Tonkin pole, leather grip, leather strap.* Bottom. *Cross-country poles, baskets, and tips. Notice that all tips are bent and point forward. Left to right: Tonkin bamboo, small basket; Tonkin bamboo, large basket; Tonkin bamboo, medium basket; fiberglass with "hoof" basket (racing pole); fiberglass touring pole, medium basket.*

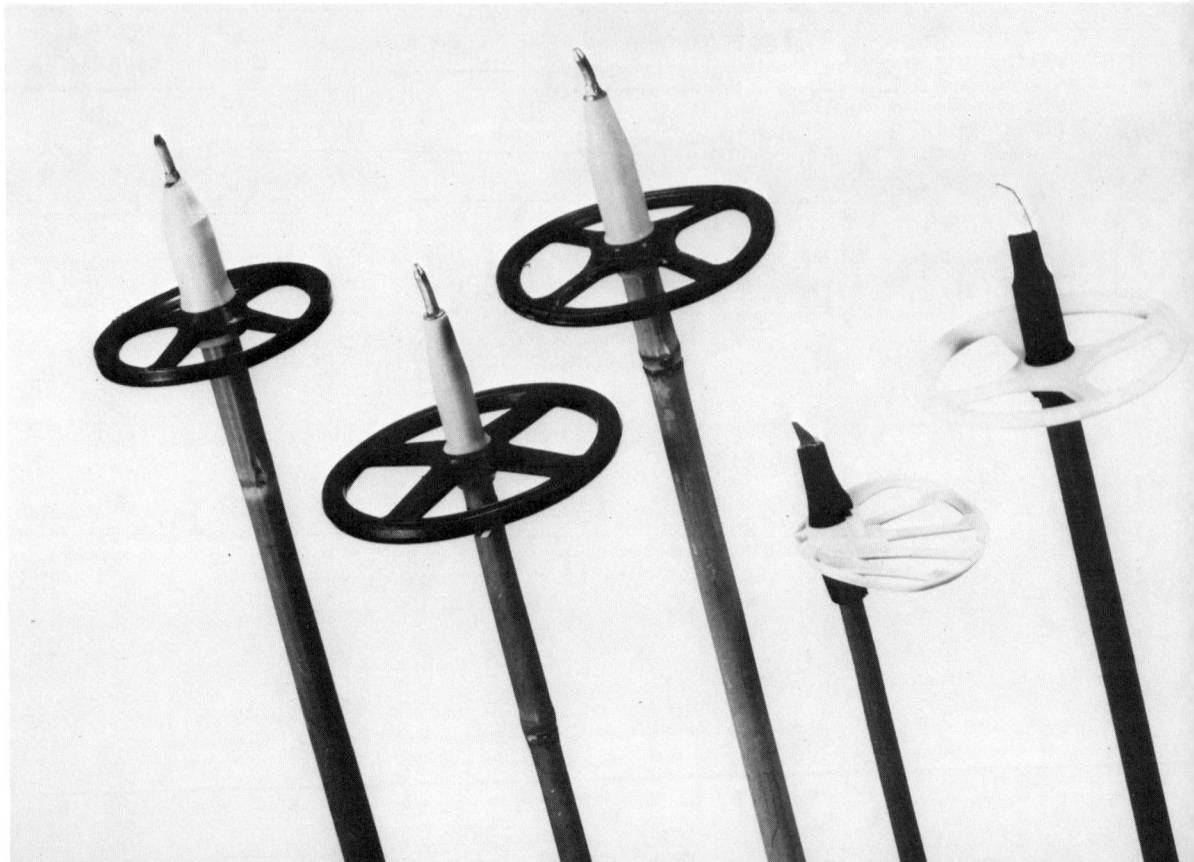

Best and final advice: **Get good boots . . . boots that fit right.** Your ski shop will help you. Get as good or better boots than you get skis! You probably will keep your boots through several pairs of skis even though you won't "use up" or wear out your skis. You'll probably (if you're anywhere near typical) fall for new ski cosmetics in a couple of years. And who knows what they'll invent that's better than what we have now. (The new car syndrome!) But those old friends, your boots, should see you through.

POLES. Poles look simple. They're actually amazingly specialized and sophisticated. They even come in right and left, and it *does* make a difference! Most people tend to view poles as just a couple of sticks. But before we tell you more about these wonderful, underrated utensils, let's get you some that are the right size.

Here's a little chart that is pretty accurate.

Your Height	Pole Length
5'–5'4"	125 cm
5'6"	130 cm
5'7"	135 cm
5'8"	135 cm
5'9"	140 cm
5'10"	140 cm
5'11"	145 cm
6'	145 cm
6'1"	150 cm
6'2"	150 cm
6'3" & over	155 cm

Your pole handles should be about as high as the head of your humerus (the knob at the front of your shoulder) when they are standing on their points on the floor. You might read or be told that poles should fit "comfortably" under your outstretched arms or be just long enough to tuck into your armpits. That's *too short* for touring poles.

Pole length is the only thing, in my mind, that is critical within 5 cm either way. Too short and they won't do what they are supposed to do, which will put you at a disadvantage. Too long and they will give you a "new muscle" every time you ski . . . sore arms in the triceps area, the backs of your upper arms.

You can't use downhill poles any more than you can use downhill skis or boots. They're too short, and the new ones don't even have straps! At the beginning of Hour 2, I'll show you how to "wear" your pole straps correctly (and tell you why). But you must get long, cross-country poles with *adjustable* straps.

Poles currently are available in Tonkin bamboo, fiberglass, aluminum, and graphite. Get bamboo or fiberglass. Aluminum poles are nice and light, but they're cold! Graphite poles are strong, whippy, light, and cost just a little more than solid gold poles of comparable length; leave them for the racers who need them. Bamboo, usually fire-tempered Tonkin, is the cheapest and really does the job well enough for almost anybody. Fiberglass poles are stronger than bamboo, generally a little more flexible, and are now coming down in price to an affordable range. It's your choice. I have and use both—and tend to like the one I'm using at the time. I've never broken a pole, but my classes average about one broken pole per day.

Cross-country pole baskets are frequently bigger than downhill baskets (which are tending toward jazzy shapes these days). Baskets keep the poles from sinking too far into the snow. Lots of hoof-shaped racing baskets (or half-baskets) are showing up in the recreational sections these days, and they work fine in thin snow covers or along prepared tracks. They lack a little support, however, in deep and fresh snow. The hoof-shaped basket does have the advantage of offering considerably less resistance to pulling out of the snow as you move forward.

Cross-country poles have curved tips. The tips curve forward as you hold the poles straight up and down. This means that the tips curve *down* when the poles are out behind you, where they do their real work: propulsion, not just balance. Let me correct, once and for all, the misinformation about why the tips curve. It is for *one reason and one reason only:* so the pole won't slip when it's holding in snow way out back where it does its work! That's the only reason! Try skiing with a pair of poles that has reversed tips or no tips at all. That will make it all clear. The poles will slip and you will slip, having only about half the grip you need!

And that's about all on equipment. It's easy to get expert help where you buy or rent these days, so there's no sense reading any more about it in a book that's supposed to teach you to *ski!*

DRESSING FOR THE WEATHER. But there's not too much information available about dressing for cross-country skiing. Listen carefully here; this is important. (Clothing, by the way, is getting as fashionable as downhill garb. Even though you still can ski in your old corduroys and a couple of sweaters, now you can buy really superior stretch bib knickers, color coordinated wind shirts, and gaiters. This new stuff is expensive, but it's so comfortable that even the occasional cross-country skier probably will want to add a new garment or two to the wardrobe.)

The first rule is to dress in layers, lots of light layers. And I'll bet you can't come within a mile of guessing why. We dress in layers to stay *cool.* Period. Sweating and getting your next-to-skin layers wet can kill you. I'll tell you why in a minute. Let's get you dressed correctly first. Then I'll tell you a little about hypothermia and winter survival.

You already have everything you'll need for cross-country skiing in your dresser and closet. Men and women dress the same except for particular undergarments and style.

First Layer (top and bottom): Fishnet long underwear. The best! Find it if you can. It's getting easier to find locally and is available by mail from those popular outfitters in Maine, Washington, and Oregon, among others. It really works. Or use wool or wool-blend longies. Why wool? Wool retains some of its insulating properties even when it is wet. A soaked cotton sweatshirt won't save your life—but a wet wool shirt will!

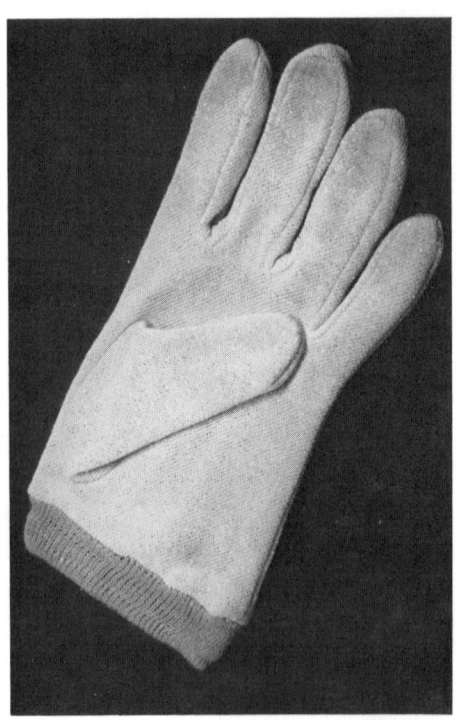

Left. *Fishnet underwear provides surprising warmth when worn with the correct outer layers.* Right. *This glove liner is very lightweight and quite warm. It has metallic fibers that reflect body heat.*

Second Layer (bottom): Knickers (if you've got them) or tightly-woven pants, waterproof or waterproofed. Old wool suit pants are good or an old pair of wool slacks or corduroys. Long bell bottoms aren't as good as short straight legs. Bells pick up snow and ice, get wet, and are generally uncomfortable.

Avoid blue jeans! They're not what you cross-country ski in. They are too stiff, not very warm, and hard to waterproof. Believe me, I've had too many "stylishly" jeaned students with wet (read "cold") seats and legs, especially on "transitional snow" days (temperature of 32 degrees or above).

Second Layer (top): Over the fishnet, wear a light, tightly-knit garment. A heavy cotton-blend turtleneck or a wool-blend jersey will do beautifully. Over regular longies, wear a wool sweater.

Third Layer (top): Add another wool sweater or, even better, a heavyweight wool shirt or shirt-jacket that either buttons or zips up.

Fourth Layer (top): A shell parka, waterproof windbreaker, or wind shirt.

Top Top Layer: A down vest, light down jacket, or other lightweight, warm garment. You'll use this mostly when you stop. Downhill ski jackets are probably too warm.

Now, all of you winter-'fraid people, please listen. Avoid: snorkle coats, overcoats, and other heavy winter garments. *Under no circumstances* should you wear a raincoat or a snowmobile suit as a warmth-producing garment—you'll sweat yourself to death!

Socks: Two pairs (no more, no less). The bottom pair can be silk (best), light wool (good), or light cotton. The top pair should be heavy wool or wool-blend. No 100 percent nylon! (And ladies— *no* pantyhose!)

Gloves/Mittens: Waterproof mittens are the best. Lined leather gloves are okay. Knit mittens work, but they do get wet. *Always* have an extra pair of hand coverings along, even when learning or on a short tour. "Glove liners" are great, take up little room in your pocket, and frequently are all you need after you get warmed up and skiing. They're available at most ski shops.

A Hat! You *must* wear a hat. Sure, you might get warm enough to take it off, but start with a hat on. The best type is a single-layer knit ski hat. (Go buy a crazy one as your "cross-country ski hat"!)

If you're a person who says, "My feet are always cold," I'll bet you also say, "I never wear a hat!" It usually works together. If your feet are cold, *put on your hat!* I'm not kidding. An uncovered head allows up to 30 percent of your body heat to escape. You get cold because your body can't produce heat as fast as it leaks away. Your feet (and hands) get cold because the heat that you are generating is being diverted from your arms and legs in the body's attempt to keep the central core and head warm. Stop that leak on top with a hat. You'll see why before we reach the end of this hour.

EXTRAS. Sunglasses (green or gray lenses); suntan/wind lotion; lip protection; a good, big handkerchief! (Your nose always seems to run when you're out in all that fresh, cold air.)

I carry a "fanny pack" (a soft day pack works just as well) with an extra pair of dry socks (light), an extra pair of gloves, and a plastic bottle of water (at least a pint). It continues to surprise me how dry I get during a tour. We just don't think as much about thirst in the winter and we *must*. My pack of "extras" usually includes: a small bag of "gorp" (nuts, raisins, dried fruits, M & Ms, chocolate bits, and granola all mixed up together . . . delicious); a scout knife; a combination screwdriver; a small pair of pliers; some nylon line; matches; compass; a whistle; my little first-aid kit; 20¢ for a phone call; and a plastic ski tip. That's my survival kit, and whenever I use anything, I replace it before my next class or tour. Skiers should have one similar kit per family.

SURVIVAL. Now, why do we wear all those layers? As I said, to stay cool! We expend a huge number of calories when we ski. That's why we almost always feel perfectly comfortable while we're skiing; but we have to work to stay *dry*. We can open or remove layers as we warm up and close or add layers as we cool off (especially when we stop to rest). A damp T-shirt or long underwear top can chill you in minutes when you stop—even if you've closed up. Regulate your clothing as you go along to avoid sweating!

As a rule, I always start by wearing one *more* layer than I think I'll need when I teach a class (and suggest that you do, too) and one *less* layer than I think I'll need when I'm just out on tour (though I have extra layers along).

Within one-half mile when on tour I always warm up enough to be comfortable, and I usually can remove my gloves within a mile. My bare hands stay warm as long as I'm moving (unless I crash), and they serve as a good reminder to add layers when I stop because they cool off *very* fast.

Dressing this way is the key to survival and is what helps us actually enjoy ourselves. Dressing wrong or not paying attention is an invitation to trouble. And trouble in the winter can

1.

be spelled H-Y-P-O-T-H-E-R-M-I-A! Nasty subject . . . and worse if it happens! Let me spend five minutes telling you what it is, how to recognize its onset, and what to do about it. I don't want to scare you or turn you off on winter, but you should know how to guard against hypothermia for your own protection—like wearing a life jacket when sailing. Incidentally, hypothermia rarely happens to cross-country skiers and never to cross-country skiers when they're actually skiing!

"Exposure." Ever read about somebody dying of exposure? He probably died of hypothermia, the cooling of the central body core. It happens in stages, usually to someone who is sedentary, such as a duck hunter who must sit quietly for hours on end. More hypothermia deaths occur, by the way, when the temperature is between 30 and 50 degrees Fahrenheit than at any other temperatures. Did you know that you can "freeze to death" when the temperature is above freezing?

The first sign is cold hands, feet, nose, and ears. The second sign is shivering. Third: deep, racking shivering, with teeth chattering. (We're getting into the danger area.) Fourth: the shivering stops! (Now we're in trouble but usually don't know it.) Next, there is a gradual loss of motor functions—poor coordination and loss of sensitivity (doesn't notice the cold anymore, inability to recognize familiar faces, etc.). Finally, there is loss of interest in everything, loss of consciousness (sleep), loss of life!

Hypothermia can happen fast. You can be in trouble within 15 minutes of the onset. Death from hypothermia can take place within half an hour (in extreme cases)!

What to do? Never ignore shivering! If you start to shiver, do one or more of the following: end the exposure (best) by going inside and getting warm; get into dry clothing—take off wet things and pile on all the dry layers you have; build a fire carefully; drink hot liquids such as coffee, tea, hot chocolate, or hot water (but *not* brandy or any other alcoholic beverage); eat candy, gorp, or something else high in calories; keep moving, exercise. For us, it means get up and get skiing again.

If you find someone who has hypothermia, you must get him warmed up as soon as possible. The best ways are in a warm room, a warm (102–105 degrees) tub of water (just the body; allow arms and legs to hang out of the tub), or a dry sleeping bag, with wet clothing removed.

That's enough of that, but you get the point, I think. It can be a hostile environment out there. Even if we're perfectly comfortable, respect winter. Better yet, stay a little afraid of it—and stay alive.

By the way, in thousands of hours of cross-country skiing and teaching, in all kinds of groups (including some with folks who were totally unprepared to be outside), and in all kinds of weather (even one course when the warmest it got was −5 degrees F) I've never even *seen* frostbite.

Frostbite shows up first in cheeks, nose, fingertips, and toes. The affected area usually takes on a white, waxy look and becomes numb. Frostbite usually does not cause pain at first. Later . . . WOW! Under no circumstances should you rub frostbite to "warm" it and *never* rub with snow (horrible old wives' tale). Warm the frostbitten part to thaw it and avoid re-freezing. It's better to let it stay frozen while getting back to camp than to thaw and risk re-freezing on the trek back.

FINDING YOUR PLACE TO LEARN. To end this hour on an up note and to get you ready for your first big hour on the snow, we have to find a place for you to take your lessons. The best place is close by, a location that you can *walk* to from home. A park, a school playground or unused athletic field, a golf course, forest preserve, vacant lot, or even a road right-of-way will do for the flatland part of the course. It should be at least 100 yards long and as close to flat as possible. It also should be a place where the tracks you make can go undisturbed for several hours (that's asking a lot).

For the hill sessions, look for a small, smooth hill. The vertical drop (total hill height) doesn't have to be more than 15 or 20 feet, and there should be a big, flat run-out area at the bottom. Even a construction site can provide a hill big enough for you to learn the turns, but a hill with cut grass under the snow is the best of all. If you get into your car to find your "schoolroom," try to find a hill and a flat area close together so you don't have to move between hours. Oh, yes. A valley is a perfectly good "hill," and the bottom of that little valley could very well be your flatland. Hope that gives you an idea of where to go.

If you go far from home, heed the advice of the U.S.S.A. (United States Ski Association). Never ski alone. Even when you go out to learn, file a "flight plan" with a friend or neighbor who can check if you're not home in a couple of hours. *Neat trick:* invite someone out to "watch your progress."

CONDITIONING. If you're concerned about starting special exercises to get ready, forget it. I think that's absolutely the best part of this sport. The best exercise for cross-country skiing is . . . cross-country skiing! Jogging or running improves your wind and stamina, but other than that, just get out and go. The more you do, the faster you become able to do more! (That sounds simplistic but it's true!) Cross-country skiing uses *all* the muscle groups, and it's a perfect exercise for the cardiovascular system. Post-cardiac therapy often recommends cross-country skiing! Olympic Nordic competitors have the lowest at-rest heartbeats of any athletes. There are some documented instances of heartbeats as low as 24 and 25 beats per minute!

You *are* going to get very tired during the course—probably much more so than on your first tours. I'm going to ask you to repeat some of these exercises time after time to get yourself trained. It's important to get the moves working well enough so you don't have to repeat the steps "1-2-3-4" in your mind.

Please do the repeats! I've experimented, been tougher on one group, easier on another, and I think I've arrived at the least number of repetitions that will get you "grooved." Besides, you *said* you wanted to learn, didn't you? You're in my class now so you're doing it, along with everybody else. I do everything I ask you to do . . . every time! I find that I actually ski one and a half times or twice as far as my students do in each class. Back and forth, uphill and down, coaching, teasing, pleading, showing off—it's how I get my little enjoyment. And I get much more tired teaching than I do just touring with family or friends.

I've included a timecheck at the end of each hour. (For Hour 1 it is simply a checklist.) Next to each item is the approximate amount of time it takes my "average" student to master the technique with the help of instructor and staff. It is harder to learn from a book, so I've added time to compensate.

You are now in class. Do everything I tell you, in order, and today you will be cross-country skiing! See you on the snow.

Hour 1.   Checklist

☐   Ski Length _____

☐   Boot Size _____

☐   Pole Length _____

☐   Dressed in Layers

_____

_____

_____

☐   "Survival Kit"

_____

_____

☐   Found My "Classroom"

Location _____

Hour 2.

✳ GETTING YOUR SKIS ON

✳ HOW TO HOLD YOUR POLES

✳ THE POSTURE

✳ STANDING STEP TURN

✳ BASIC FORWARD SHUFFLE

✳ FALLING AND GETTING UP

✳ STRAIGHT DOWNHILL RUNNING

Hour 2.

DOING IT OUTSIDE

✳

WELCOME TO THE SNOW. LET'S SPEND FIVE MINUTES GETTING OUR GEAR ON THE CORRECT HANDS AND FEET, AND THEN WE'LL GET ON WITH SKIING.

We'll assume that everyone has his boots on the intended feet and proceed right to the skis themselves.

GETTING YOUR SKIS ON. Look at the bindings. All Nordic Norm 3-pin bindings have some sort of markings for right and left on them. Some have a little triangular hole on the outside of the part of the binding that goes under the sole of your boot. Some have the words "right" or "left," some have a little square hole in the bale catch mechanism or an arrow, and some even have a little symbol of a bare foot with tiny toes. Get your bindings on the correct feet. It *is* possible to put them on wrong, but your heels will keep slipping off the insides, heel plate or not.

Oh, yes, about heel plates. Make sure the skis you rent have them, and insist that the skis you buy are equipped with them before you try to ski. Heel plates keep you from slipping around on top of your skis. They're very important. They should be positioned so you can get a good "full heel" on them. As I mentioned earlier, my 10-year-old son likes to use a pair of my 210 cm ultra-light "racing training" skis sometimes, so I added another set of heel plates that fit his boots, too. (He has *no* trouble with skis that long; it would be like me using 280s or 300 cm skis!)

When you've figured out right and left, unlatch the bale and slide your boot all the way onto the binding. The three pins will snuggle into the three holes in the boot sole. Gently twist your

Top. Nordic Norm bindings and boots. These have a little triangle on the outside of each binding. Both boots and bindings flare more to the outside. Pins in the bindings fit into holes in boot sole. Bottom. Getting your bindings on. With bale up, push your boot all the way forward.

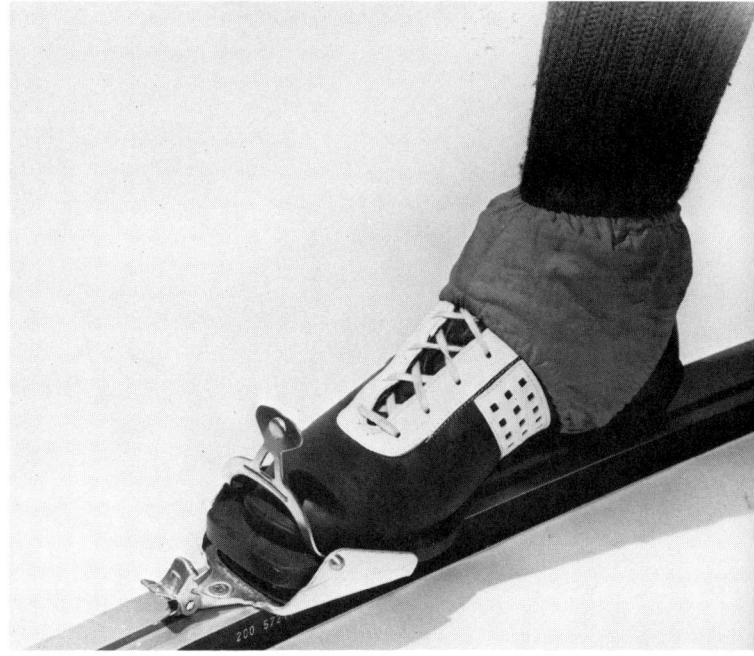

Lift your heel; it helps the pins seat in the holes. Then fasten the bale with the catch (some can be done with your pole), and you're ready to ski!

foot around until the pins are "home," and then lock the bale down over the top of the extended front part of your boot sole. Most bindings nowadays can be snap-locked with your pole tip, but some still must be fastened by hand. Both styles hold perfectly, so it's a matter of choice (and what the shop you deal with sells).

The newest nylon bindings lock and release with a simple kick of your boot or the edge of your ski. But until it's second nature, you might wish to kneel down and "help" them with your hands. Most bindings have two or three lock positions. Generally, the first one that holds is all you need. If you have trouble with even the first notch, try lifting your heel two or three inches. It will help to keep the pins seated while you fasten.

HOW TO HOLD YOUR POLES. This is important! Your pole straps *do most of the work*, so learn from the first moment to use them correctly. I continually run into two people who ski "every day" but who have their straps taped down. After two years, on and off, of trying to convince them, I've finally shut up. They must want to work that much harder and that much less efficiently!

Your hands should come up through the straps and down over both sides. The strap goes around the back of your hand, where it will do most of the pulling, around the base of your thumb and heel of your hand, and, coming together, up between your thumb and index finger. In other words, your hand will hold down the strap.

The strap should be tight enough so that only one inch of it is visible (from where it comes into sight behind your hand to where it disappears into the pole handle). To make sure you're wearing your poles right, let them hang by the straps from your wrists; then put your hands down over the straps, holding both sides of each strap between your hand and the pole grip. You'll see that you hardly have to hang on with your hands, that your forearms never tire, that you can use your poles way out behind you for that extra push, and that the straps always keep the grips exactly where you want them, uphill or down.

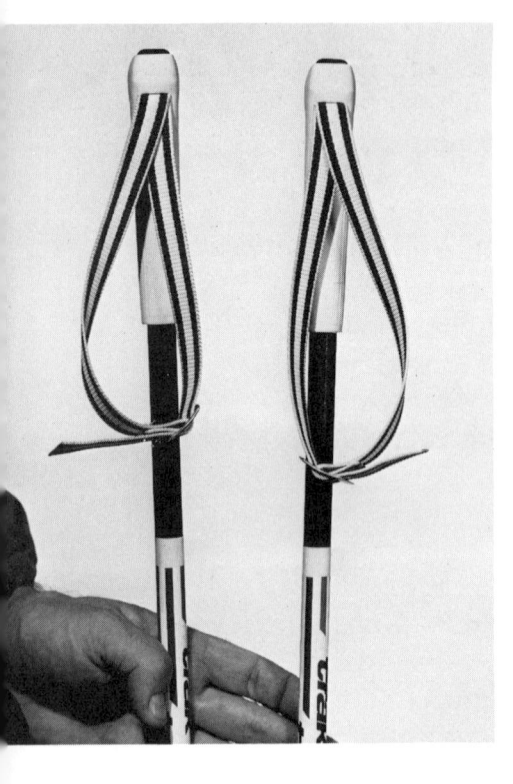

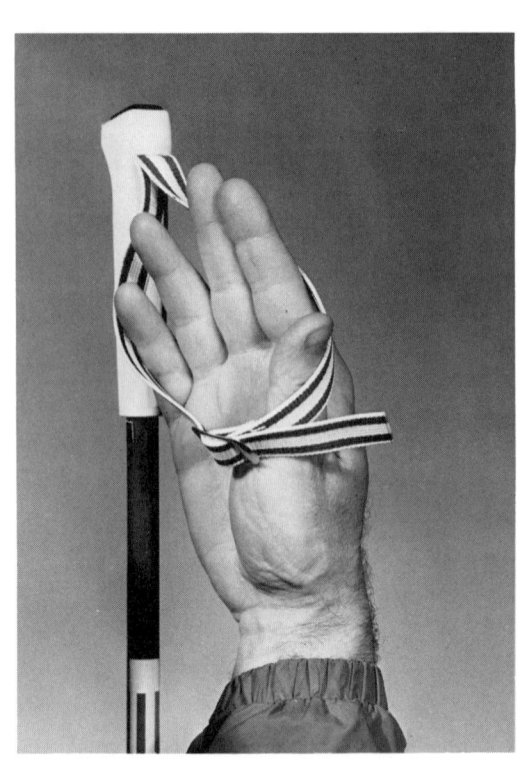

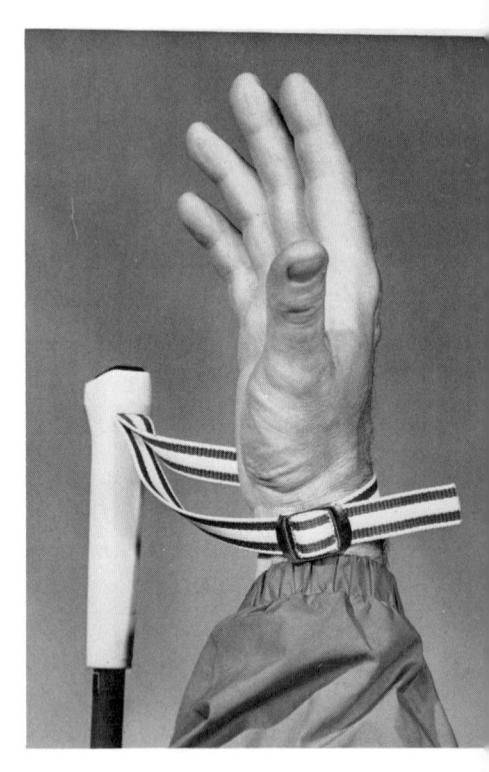

Yes, there really are right and left poles! The bottom strap on each side hangs to the inside. Make sure you get a pair when you buy.

How to put on your poles: Put your hand up through the strap . . . all the way through. Let the poles hang on your wrists and now bring your hand down over both straps. Both sides come up your palm. When you've got them on right, your thumb will hold down the bottom strap.

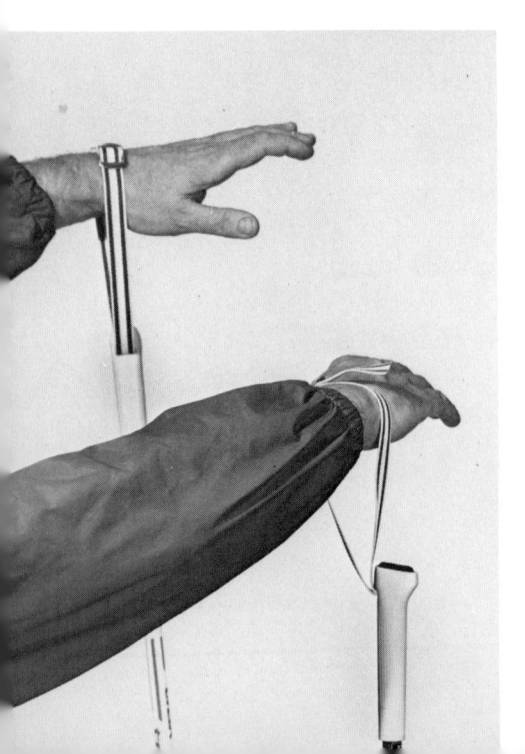

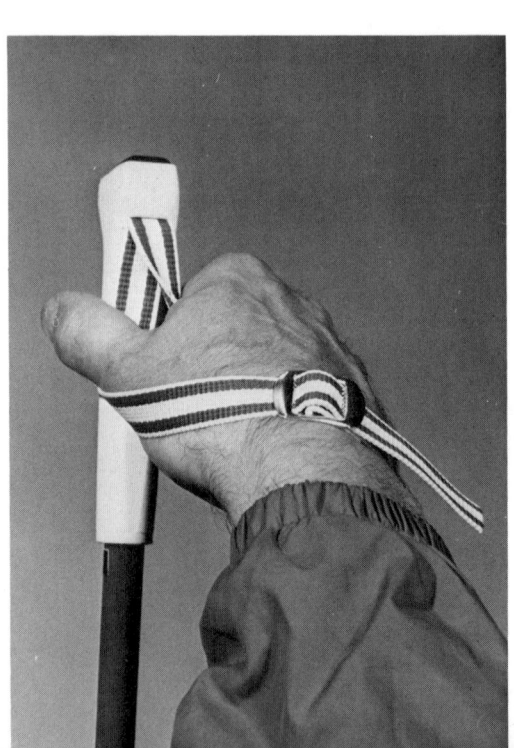

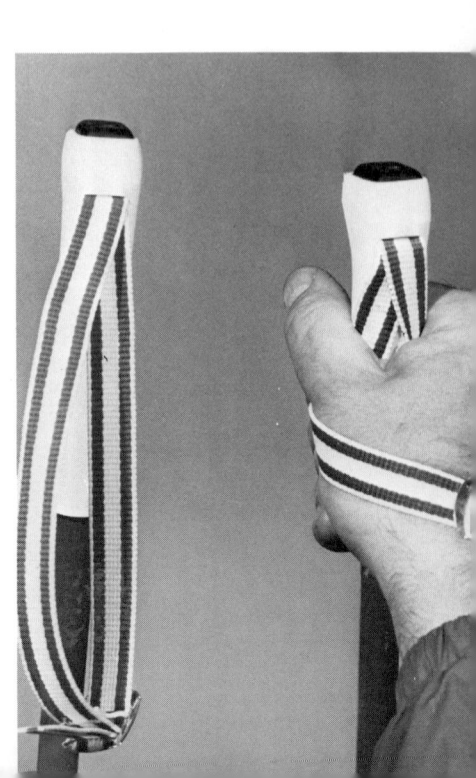

The Posture. Head up, knees unlocked, back straight and relaxed.

This first day it really doesn't make that much difference, but as I told you when you were "fitting out," there is a right and a left pole. The trick for determining which is which is that your thumb holds down the bottom strap when you have the pole on correctly. I mark my right one, even though I can tell by feel.

Skis on. Poles on. Now you're ready to go. Just remember that caution from our "getting dressed" section. You'll probably want to wear one more layer while you're learning than you'll be comfortable with when you're actually touring. I always start touring one layer "underdressed" (but I have that layer along) because I warm up in five minutes or so and find that I'm perfectly comfortable. When I teach, I always have on one extra layer—I stand around more, too!

THE POSTURE. To get ready to ski, all you have to do is *unlock* your knees, look up (straight ahead), and shuffle away. It's not a deep knee bend or even a half bend; just keep your knees unlocked and off you go. The more time you spend with your back naturally straight and your legs as straight as possible, the less tired you're going to be at the end of your outing. Now and forevermore.

Q. How far apart should my feet be?
A. How far apart *are* your feet? The way you naturally stand/walk is right for you. Usually, there will be three to six inches

Standing Step Turn, or "Making a Flower." Follow the picture sequence and notice that my left foot is "making a fist" in my boot and that the tail of the moving ski is down hard on the snow. Turning the full 360 degrees makes our "flower" in the snow.

between the ankles. You'll find that's about how far apart the "tracks" are that you'll follow (and that you'll make yourself).

With your knees unlocked, your eyes straight ahead and looking at least at the horizon, and a smile on your face, you're ready to begin your forward shuffle. You're going to need a relatively flat stretch at least 100 yards long. This can be in the woods, in a park, on a golf course, or even next to the highway—anywhere flat, where the tracks you make can stay untrampled for a couple of hours. We'll be coming back to use these tracks later. Sometimes in class we use a rectangular "course," but that's mostly because the coaches can stand in the middle and help students as they go around. Lazy!

Now we're going to shuffle along for 100 yards or so, turn around, and come back.

STANDING STEP TURN.

Q. Wait a minute. How do you turn around on these things?
A. Okay, before we start, I'd better show you the *standing step turn*. This is one of those things that you have to master early because it constitutes the basis of a more complex maneuver that we'll learn in the third hour.

We're going to make some "flowers" in the snow while we turn around a full 360 degrees in both directions, slowly but surely. Lean back just a little on your heels, pulling up with your toes. The tops of your boots should bulge. Shift your weight onto one ski, and pivot the other ski outward, away from the weighted one, about 10 to 14 inches. Now shift your weight onto the ski you just moved, and close 'em up by scissoring the first ski around parallel to the one your weight's on now. The tails of your skis must stay firmly pressed into the snow. You must *not* pick up the entire ski; you're not "stepping around" but rather "scissoring" around, pivoting with those tails jammed down on the snow.

Pulling up with your toes and keeping your ankles "strong" accomplishes the turn. When you do it right, all the way around, you'll make a "flower" pattern in the snow, with the ski tails

Forward Shuffle. Eyes up, and slide your skis forward. Avoid walking and just slide, slide, slide. It's very easy and natural.

staying in the exact center. Keep those tails down; don't fake it! It's easy, so do it right from the beginning—both to the right and to the left.

BASIC FORWARD SHUFFLE. Now we're ready to ski. The first time you go down your 100 yards, you're probably going to be "breaking trail," so the going will be slow.

Q. How do I keep going in a perfectly straight line?
A. The same way you steer a straight course in a sailboat. Pick a "landmark," a tree or bush, and keep heading straight for it. You'll zigzag a little, but soon you'll be able to carve a pretty straight track.

At the end of your 100-yard trek, make "half a flower" either to the right or left and come back in your own tracks. Your smile should really be working now. It's much easier the second and each subsequent time . . . skiing in a nice, straight, packed trail. Keep your head up, and try to slide your skis. You're not walking now. The basic shuffle is much closer to ice skating than to anything else. You'll probably notice that you're dipping slightly with each slide, and that's perfectly right. Your poles will automatically be working opposite your feet, just as your right arm and left leg move together when you walk . . . and for the same reason: balance.

Shuffling Without Poles. By gosh, I can move forward without my poles. I may learn to do this yet!

Q. How do I keep the ski tips from spreading apart (doing the splits) or crossing as I go down the track?
A. If they do, I can tell that you've probably been fudging and looking at your ski tips as you go along! Look up . . . farther. Concentrate on sliding your feet/legs in a straight line and following through with your body. The shuffle is an acquired skill, and in an hour or less you'll hardly believe you ever asked such a question.

Now turn and travel back down your tracks again, smoothly. Try to get a little rhythm working. It's easy and kind of fun. You're not in a race, so go gently but firmly—be a little aggressive. Work on getting a little glide at the end of each slide, not too much yet, just six inches or a foot. Remember, that glide is "free" travel . . . what touring is all about. By the end of the six hours, you should be getting two or three feet—or even more—of free travel with each kick.

We'll go four trips this way, two up and two back, and then you will be ready for the first of my many little surprises. Slip your hands out of your pole straps and *Park Your Poles!*

Q. How can I move without my poles?
A. Easy! At this point they're just a crutch. Cross-country is truly a "leg" sport, and it's actually easier at this stage *without* your poles.

Now make two round trips "without." You really should feel "unencumbered" about the middle of your first trip, and the first time you feel the freedom, you'll know that you're actually cross-country skiing—in only 15 short minutes of the first hour!

After your two round trips—up, back, up, and back—you're ready to pick up the poles again (get those straps on correctly) and head for a little practice hill. I hope it is fairly close by. It needn't have a vertical drop of more than 10 or 15 feet for this phase of your learning. It is important, though, that there be a clear run-out area at the bottom because we don't want to think about stopping yet. Remember, a valley is a hill (of sorts), too.

The hill I use for most of my teaching has a drop of about 25 feet, but it's amazing how much "downhill" you can learn in such a short run.

As an aside, you'll notice that we spend a lot of time going downhill . . . and you thought cross-country was a flatland sport. Well, it is and it isn't! You're going to come across uphills and downhills on every tour. You can't let a little drop scare you or slow you down. I've found that I can build confidence faster on these little bunny hills than anywhere else . . . you'll see.

On our way to the hill, let's take a minute to cover another one of those necessary basics: getting up after you fall. (Not *if* you fall but *when* you fall.)

FALLING AND GETTING UP. Our lightweight, flexible equipment with toe bindings and loose heels makes the problem of getting up after a fall a simple matter rather than one of acrobatics, yoga, or brute strength.

You *must* fall and learn to get up your first time out. You surely will fall sometime on the trail, everybody does occasionally, and the time to learn to get up is at the outset rather than after you find yourself stuck. Obviously, you always can snap open one or both bindings, but it's hardly ever necessary (even if you are of advanced age, stiff, or partially handicapped).

First, standing on your skis with bindings fastened, discard your poles and gently drop to your hands and knees. Crawl forward a few feet. It's almost as if you had nothing attached to your feet! Now kneel straight up, slide one leg forward, and just stand up! You've learned the secret: "If you can get to your knees, you can get up." Now let's take it from a spill.

This time, poles on, skis on, just "let the air out of your knees" and slowly sink sideways until you tumble over in the snow. Hug your sides with your arms, and put both poles out to the side opposite the one on which you're about to fall. Avoid putting a hand out to slow yourself. Just fall flat onto the snow on your upper arm, shoulder, and hip. Pick a nice soft patch of snow for your first tumble and you'll be surprised at how little it hurts. (In fact, it feels pretty good to just lie there for a minute.)

Now roll over on your back and kick your feet/skis above your head. It's easy to do since the skis weigh almost nothing. When they're waving around up there parallel to each other, just roll your body, legs, and skis to one side or the other. Keep the skis parallel, and as they come down toward the snow, bring your knees as far forward as you can. Then continue your "roll" by pushing yourself with your "down" shoulder . . . ending up on your hands and knees again! (Remember to get one knee between the skis so you can maintain your balance.) Your poles should not be in the way at all, and there's no need to take them off. Then stand up, just as before.

Falling and Getting Up. Practice on the flat. First, "let the air out of your knees"; sink down and fall over. Notice the "elbow and pole tuck."

Falling and Getting Up (cont.). Now, roll on your back. Kick your skis up in the air and wave them around. They're light and very controllable. Next, after you've rolled back down and over onto your hands and knees, plant your poles, kneel upright with one knee on the snow between your skis, and up you go.

2.

That's all there is to falling and getting up . . . on the flat. But there are two more things you must know about getting back to your feet after a tumble on a hill. First, your skis must lie straight *across* the hill. If they're pointing too far uphill or downhill, you're in for a little surprise—you'll be skiing again before you're halfway up and before you're ready. Second, your skis must be downhill from your body. With these two conditions satisfied, just follow the same procedures you took on the flat and . . . you're skiing again.

If you have terrible trouble with the "roll up," here's an alternative. Take your hand out of the uphill strap. Hold both poles together, with your downhill hand on the tops of both poles and your uphill hand on both baskets (the poles cross in front of your body, from upper downhill to lower uphill). Now, just "lever" yourself to your knees and stand up (remember to keep one knee between the skis).

If you've fallen like a "bundle of sticks," your skis every which way, the "roll over" onto your back will remedy the "knot." The more you get used to being down and getting up, the more it becomes second nature. Soon you'll not notice your frequent little crashes, won't even remember them. And by the time that happens, you'll probably be falling less anyway.

A frequent problem: In almost every class I have at least one student who can't get up that first time. It's usually because he is trying to get up from a sitting position and not from hands

Getting Up on a Hill. After you get your skis downhill across the fall line, slip off the strap of your uphill pole.

Getting Up on a Hill (cont.). *Put both poles together with your uphill hand on both baskets. (This keeps you from putting too much strain on just one pole.) Push yourself to your knees with one knee between your skis on the snow. Then slowly push yourself up, using both poles as a cane. Now you're ready to go.*

and knees! If you're having trouble, make sure you can crawl forward a few "steps" before you try to stand.

STRAIGHT DOWNHILL RUNNING. Now we're ready for some *fun!* We're going to slide down our little hill a couple of dozen times. We're not even going to think about stopping (until Hour 3), so let's get into the "downhill position" and go!

Downhill Posture. The downhill position on cross-country skis is simple. Bend your knees a little more than in the touring posture, getting a little spring/shock absorber into them but nothing elaborate, not a half-deep knee bend or anything. One ski will want to be about six or eight inches in front of the other. (It makes no difference which one is in front. Try it both ways to see which side you favor.) Your back will be *straight* and *relaxed;* your arms will ride at your sides, relaxed, poles trailing behind you just off the snow. Keep your head up, eyes at least at the base of the hill. You can't tense up here or you'll *make* yourself fall!

Returning Uphill. I'm going to assume that you'll have no trouble getting back up your gentle little hill. If you do, here's a tip: keep your knees bent a little; lean back (yes, *back*) on your heels; and put your poles way back behind you . . . they're *pushing* you uphill and keeping you from sliding back. If you can see your hands out of the corners of your eyes, the poles are too far forward; get them back.

Downhill Posture. Look straight ahead, with your back straight and relaxed and with some spring in your knees. Heels flat on skis.

2.

What's wrong with this picture? Knees locked; looking at skis; tense; heading for a crash.

Now shorten your shuffle and slide, slide, slide, with little short slides, quickly alternating right foot/left pole, left foot/right pole, and you'll just scoot right up the hill. You'll be able to feel that stopped ski gripping the snow. The more you lean back, the more grab you'll feel and the easier it will be. I'll cover all the uphill techniques in Hours 4 & 5.

Downhill Running. I've had hundreds of students who were scared silly of pushing off from the top of "Everest" (our 25-foot peak), and most of them fell once or twice until they finally believed me and loosened up. Here's how *not* to start downhill: Timidly push off, knees locked (or rigid), arms bent at the elbow, poles up in the air and held with typical death grip, body bent forward at the waist anywhere from a few degrees to full "bow,"* eyes on ski tips (where else), and mind focused on falling. The skier is rarely disappointed and usually falls backward within a few feet.

Q. Why do I fall backward?
A. You're leaning too far forward, getting off balance, overcompensating, and falling backward. Straighten up and loosen up.

*Just once, try walking down stairs tense and bent forward at the waist. Hold on to the banister; I don't want you to crash. You can hardly do it! You naturally descend stairs with your weight balanced, your back straight and relaxed, and your knees and upper legs absorbing all the little shocks.

I had a heavyset lady who kept falling backward and hitting her head and seeing stars. Instead of quitting, she went out and got a motorcycle helmet—and it did the trick! Almost immediately she was skiing downhill without a fall, and by the end of the six hours she was getting good half-snowplow turns and even an occasional, acceptable telemark! She loosened up as soon as she felt she wouldn't hurt herself. You do the same.

One more anecdote. One of my best students is a local minister who is totally blind to the front. He has good peripheral vision but literally cannot see to the front. He had faith in my instructions, and standing at the top of the hill (undoubtedly with additional faith as well!), he relaxed and made the bottom without a hitch. The rest of the session had him blasting back uphill and swooping down again, his characteristic and famous huge grin never leaving his face. (Come to think of it, I don't think he ever fell on the hill.)

While running downhill, keep trying to look at the horizon. I find that the less I look at the actual terrain, the more I let my legs absorb the little irregularities and my reflexes do the skiing. Sometimes I like to look straight out and enjoy the feeling of sinking down as though I were riding an escalator.

Do downhills until you can kick off aggressively and shoot to the bottom, enjoying it all the way. If you've been skiing on an unskied hill, fresh snow, try to break a slightly new trail every time down. This "grooms" the snow, and the smoother it gets, the faster it gets and the more confidence you'll have.

Once you can ski downhill time after time without drama you're ready for Hour 3 and our most demanding single skill. One final comment on downhill: if you relax, your skis will track straight and you'll have a really good time.

Hour 2.   Timecheck

- ☐ Equipment on Correctly: 5 Minutes
- ☐ Standing Step Turn: 7 Minutes
- ☐ Basic Forward Shuffle with Poles: 10 Minutes
- ☐ Basic Forward Shuffle *without* Poles: 9 Minutes
- ☐ Falling and Getting Up
    - ☐ On the Flat: 8 Minutes
    - ☐ On the Hill: 5 Minutes
- ☐ Downhill Posture: 1 Minute
- ☐ Returning Uphill: 2 Minutes
- ☐ Downhill Running: 13 Minutes

Hour 3.

✳ THE SNOWPLOW

✳ SNOWPLOW STOPS

✳ THE KICK TURN

Hour 3.

SLOWING DOWN & STOPPING

✷

NOW THAT YOU'RE A DOWNHILL "BULLET," LET'S LEARN TO STOP. THERE ARE SEVERAL WAYS OF GETTING THE JOB DONE. THE FIRST IS TO "HIT THE SILK," OR "BAIL OUT," THE SECOND IS THE SNOWPLOW (WHICH WE'RE ABOUT TO LEARN), AND THE THIRD—AND BEST—IS TO CONTROL YOUR SPEED BY TURNING.

Turning is not always practical (or even possible). Bailing out sometimes hurts your pride—and other areas (but occasionally it is the *only* way to get the job done)—so we're left with the ubiquitous snowplow. Let's start slowing down and stopping.

THE SNOWPLOW. *Fair warning:* The snowplow is the hardest single maneuver for most students. I'm going to over-describe it, or describe it more than one way, so you will get the whole idea. (P.S. It isn't *really* that hard!)

The most important thing to learn about the snowplow is that as you form the inverted "V" with your skis, a pigeon-toed position, your feet must be far enough apart so that the tips *can't* cross. And I mean your feet must be *way* apart! Three feet apart! Thirty-six inches! When you succeed in coming to a stop, you should be aware that your knees are almost locked (though you didn't start that way) and that you're pushing hard with your heels. Aggressively.

Here's how the snowplow is done. Start downhill and when you're moving, push your heels out hard, rotating your toes inward slightly. Concentrate on forcing your heels out and getting the tails of your skis four to six feet apart.

Snowplow Position. The knees drive in, edging skis slightly; feet are far enough apart so skis can't cross; heels are down hard, pushing out.

    The most common problem at this point is that the skis are not far enough apart, tips are crossing, and the student pitches forward over them. You can't ski when your tips cross. If you have trouble getting all this together at the top of the hill, try this: ski all the way down, thinking about what you're going to do, and start your snowplow at the bottom—on the flat. It will bring you to a stop quicker, build your confidence, and boost your progress.

    After your snowplow is beginning to work at the bottom of the hill, go into the plow a few feet sooner, while you are still actually on the incline. Then just keep moving your starting point uphill (backward) until you've got it working near the top.

    Your arms are used only to provide balance, and your poles are absolutely useless. In fact (oh, no!), let's park the poles again until you've got the plow all together.

    Let's try it again. Practice, incidentally, should be done in the area you've been packing down, smoothing out. If you're practicing on a different day, start by "breaking down" the hill.

1. Start downhill.
2. Push your ski *tails* out with your heels. This results in a side-slipping* action of the skis and is really quite easy once you're actually moving. Push the skis way apart, three feet apart!

*In side-slipping, your skis slide sideways while remaining flat, thus encountering almost no resistance. They do not "edge."

A frequent mistake! Concern with falling allows tips to cross, and you usually overcompensate and fall backward.

3. Now bend your knees together a little. Get a little "knock-kneed." This makes the outside edges of the skis lift off the snow slightly and the inside edges "edge," or bite, causing scraping friction.

4. "Get about 1,000 lbs. on your shoulders," and push down hard, with all your weight and with your mind! Get mean! and you'll stop! Depending on conditions, you'll either stop in a few feet, slide on a little way at first, slowing down all the time, or you might slide almost all the way down the hill if it's really packed and slick. That's okay! What we're trying to do is control our descent and stay in total charge of our skis.

SNOWPLOW STOPS. If you're generating any "stop" at all, you're probably holding your upper body in the correct position—just about straight up and down, with muscles relaxed.

3.

If you're falling every time, I can tell what you're doing wrong even though I can't see you. If you're falling forward, chances are that you're tense and not getting your feet three feet apart (yes! I really *mean* 36 inches). Your feet probably are 18 inches or so apart (common beginning posture) *and* your ski tips are crossing. Remember, your feet should be so far apart that your tips cannot cross.

If you're falling backward, you're bending forward at the waist, all tensed up, so that eventually you lose your balance, overcompensate, and end up flat on your back . . . most likely "seeing stars."

If you fall to one side or the other, you probably just caught an edge. Get up and try it again. I had one student whose ankles turned out. She got the skis almost far enough apart, but she

Snowplow Stop. Legs so far apart skis can't cross; back straight; upper body relaxed; knees driving in and skis "edged."

61

insisted on trying to dig in the outside edges of her skis! She fell every time until we finally got her to "ankle in."

Now practice, practice, practice. You should do the snowplow at least 15 times *after* you've got it. Devote at least half an hour to snowplow stopping.

By the way, if you seem to turn to one side or the other, pay it no mind. Concentrate on skiing straight, both legs doing their share of the work. We'll get to moving turns in the next hour.

Now retrieve your poles and let's do a few more stops. Your arms probably have just been hanging down or even "pushing down" without the poles. What do you suppose you do with the poles now that you're holding them? My poles just splay out behind me, providing a sort of "air brake." They usually wind up about parallel to the "snowplowed" skis below them.

The people who seem to have the most trouble mastering the snowplow stop are my gentle students. Frequently, they are women 50 and over. Here's a great tip. Be a tiger when you snowplow stop. Be really aggressive! Get mean! (even do a little growl). It helps.

And stay in control! It's your hill; you picked it. They're your skis, and they ought to do what *you* want them to do. If you're falling, you're letting the hill, the skis, or your fear of falling control you! Get tough!

Here's an easy exercise. Try to stop about four or five times. Each time, before coming to a halt, tuck the tails in again and pick up speed. If you were doing it on fresh snow, your trail would look like a series of hourglasses, as in the diagram.

Think you've got it? Then let's take a "fun break" after all that work and learn the "flashy" way to turn 180 degrees and ski back in our own tracks.

THE KICK TURN. We don't do it just because it's flashy, but that's one good reason to learn the kick turn. There are a couple of different techniques you can use. Let's do the easy one (for *me*) first, and then we'll explain the "Alpine" method.

The kick turn is used to change directions approximately 180 degrees on either the flat or hills. It's the easiest and fastest

Cross-Country Kick Turn. Notice in these sequence shots how the poles lift to let the moving ski bypass them and that the ski in the air is beginning to turn out.

way to turn around. It is also the only way to change directions if you are going uphill by one of the "traverse" methods. (See Hours 4 & 5.)

Here's how the kick turn is done—first to the right, using your poles for balance. Pick up your right ski (18–24 inches) and extend your leg forward, turning the ski out (away from the left ski) and pointing your toe. As soon as the tail clears your stationary left ankle, flip it all the way around in the air (180 degrees from the left ski). Step down on it, transferring your weight to the right ski. Your body now has turned 90 degrees to the right, and your skis are parallel again, but going in opposite directions.

Keeping your weight on the right ski, lift the left ski (just a few inches) and drag the tail around parallel to the right (same direction), as your body continues its turn around the final 90 degrees. You must lift your poles and put them back down, keeping them out of the way of the swinging skis and maintaining your balance as your body swings through the 180 degrees. A turn to the left is done the same way, but to the opposite side, beginning with the left ski and turning it out!

The most common mistakes in the beginning are turning the raised ski across the other (turning *in* instead of *out*), trying to do a "high kick" and losing your balance, and tripping over your poles by doing a "wooden soldier," tensed-up turn.

Look at the pictures on page 63 and try to get yourself into the same positions. The smooth swing of your body is the key, along with the progressive circular movement of your weight from one pole to the other. To the right again, it's:

1. Kick right leg up and forward, clearing the left ankle with the right ski tail.
2. Lift both poles, and swing your upper body 90 degrees to the right.
3. Continue the swing of the right ski until it is 180 degrees around from the left one.
4. Transfer your weight onto the right ski while you . . .
5. Plant the right pole to the outside of the left ski tail.
6. With the right pole and right ski providing support, lift your left ski a little bit (less than one foot) and drag the tail around until the left ski is once again parallel to the right ski and facing in the same direction.
7. Your body has continued its smooth swing around to the right, and you now are facing in the new direction, ready to go as . . .
8. Your left pole plants next to the repositioned left ski.

3.

If you got that wrong at about Step 5, you now look like a pretzel. Have someone help you get unwound and try it again.

You'll need to do the kick turn in both directions when we start our uphill traverses, so work it out right now. Yes, your legs *will* let you get into that halfway around position.

Once you finally learn the kick turn and get it grooved, it's like having learned to ride a bicycle. It's suddenly so easy that you can't imagine why initially you had trouble.

Here's the way they teach "downhillers" to do the same turn with their "iron maiden" boots and rigid bindings. If you've had a little problem with the "easy way," try it this Alpine way and maybe you'll feel better. To the right again:

1. Kick your right foot/ski forward and flip the tail down so it actually sticks in the snow. It should be stuck down opposite the shovel of your left ski, about 8 to 10 inches to the right of it.
2. Your poles are out almost at arms' length and stuck in the snow for stability.
3. Now pivot the right ski to the right, around the tail, which is stuck in the snow. Turn the tip *down* to the right, while smoothly turning your upper body one-quarter turn to the right.
4. Step onto the right ski as it rotates down onto the snow. You now have one ski facing "north" and one ski facing "south."
5. Your right pole was lifted, moved, and planted again outside of the tail of your not-yet-moved left ski as it made way for the descending right ski and as your shoulders did their quarter-turn.
6. Now lift your pole and left ski and continue your body's swing to the right, the second quarter-turn. Plant the left pole in its new, all-the-way-around position.
7. Drag the left ski around into place, threading it inside the planted left pole.
8. Ski away. Smiling.

Ideally, this move is very smooth, and when the second ski comes around, you actually can get a little kick, enabling you to move immediately off in the new direction.

Practice, practice, practice. And since we're going to be spending most of the next two hours on the hill, try your kick turn

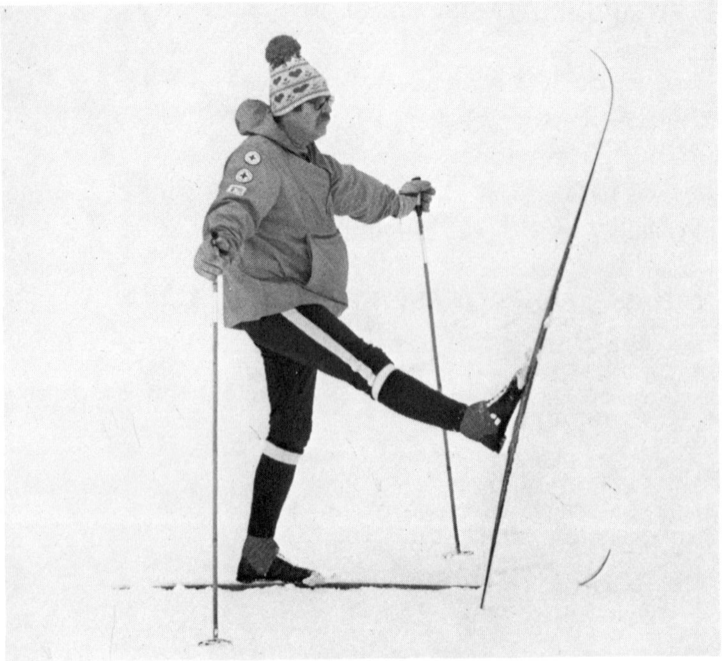
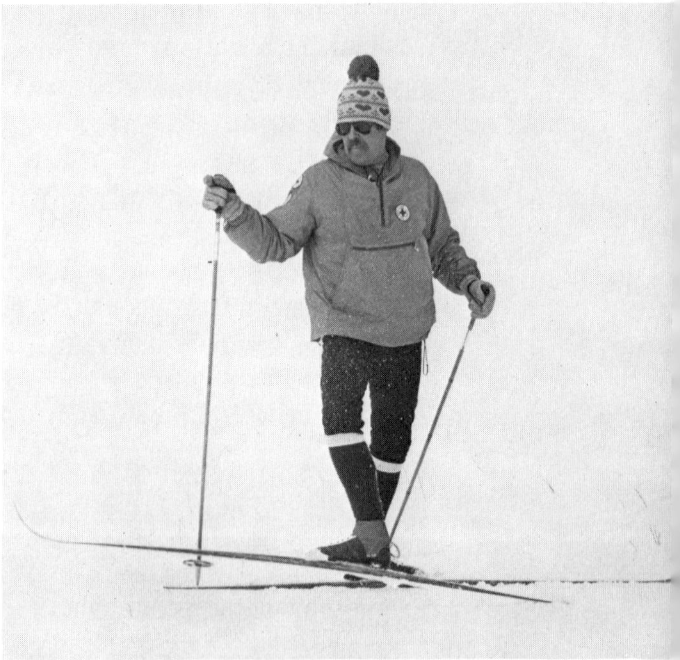
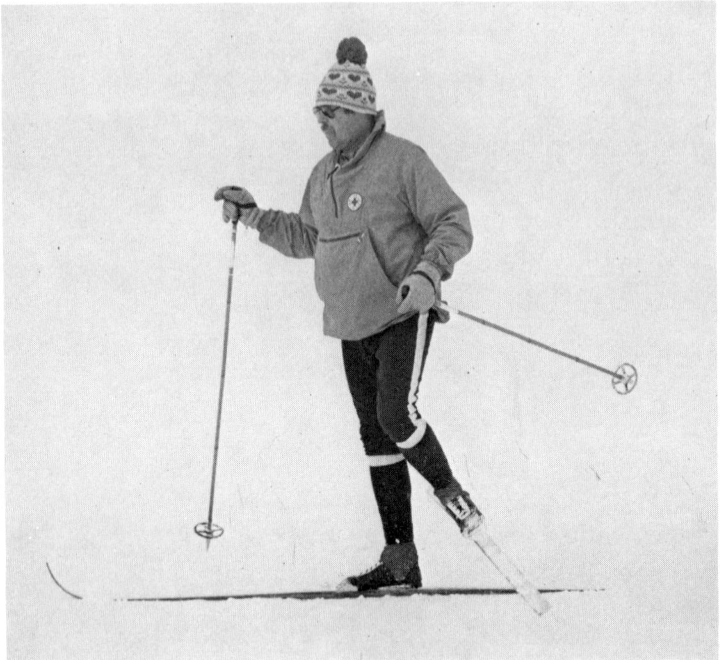
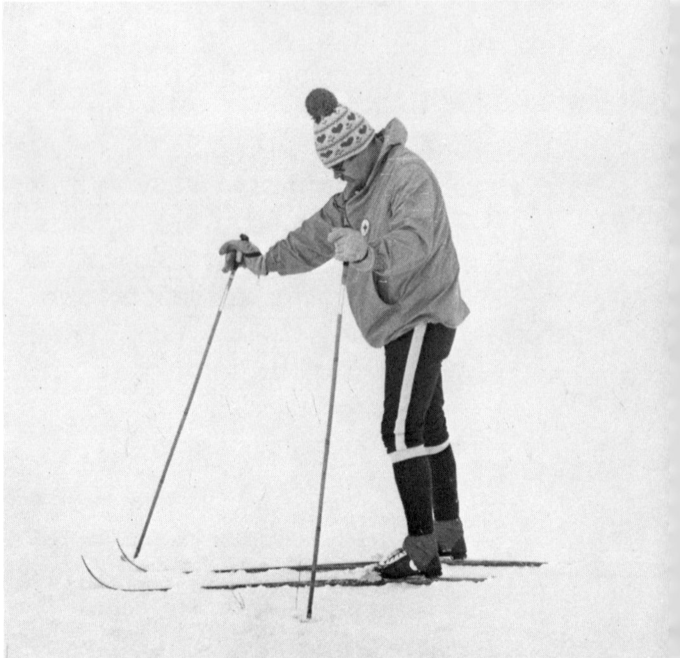

on the hill . . . pick a spot about halfway up.

Remember, the kick turn is used for changing directions *across* the hill. It cannot be used for changing from straight uphill to straight downhill in the middle of the hill. Try it and see why.

When kick turning on the hill, you'll want to turn the *uphill* ski first most of the time. Later, when you've really got your confidence, you can turn down. You'll find that it will start you skiing downhill, which is okay if you're prepared and in control.

Now, let's head for the top of the hill and learn our turns.

3.

"Alpine" Kick Turn. Kick up and plant that tail in the snow. Then just turn it out, step it down, and lift the other ski around.

Hour 3. Timecheck

- [ ] Snowplow Position: 5 Minutes
    - [ ] Feet Far Enough Apart
- [ ] Snowplow Stops: 35 Minutes
- [ ] "Hourglass" Exercise: 5 Minutes
- [ ] The Kick Turn
    - [ ] Flat: 10 Minutes
        - [ ] Right
        - [ ] Left
    - [ ] Hill: 5 Minutes
        - [ ] Right
        - [ ] Left

Hours 4.&5.

✳ HALF-SNOWPLOW TURNS

✳ LINKED HALF-SNOWPLOW TURNS

✳ MOVING STEP TURNS

✳ SKATING TURNS

✳ UPHILL SIX WAYS

Hours 4.&5.

DOWNHILL TURNS & SIX WAYS UPHILL

✳

AT THIS POINT, WE'RE JUST UNDER HALFWAY THROUGH THE COURSE, AND YOU'RE READY FOR A TOUR. IT WOULD HELP YOUR SKIING IF YOU WOULD DETOUR THROUGH THE WOODS FOR A COUPLE OF MILES BEFORE WE START OUR TURN SERIES. WE'LL BE WORKING PRETTY HARD FOR AN HOUR AND A HALF OR TWO HOURS, SO IT WON'T HURT TO GET WARMED UP A BIT.

We spend about three-quarters of our total six hours learning time going downhill and back up again. It should be obvious why you have to learn several techniques and gain lots of confidence in your new abilities: to be ready for that first hill (up or down) on your first tour.

Most of us ski tourers spend most of our touring time on relatively flat terrain, and the prudent distance skier will try to conserve energy by going around the hills rather than just doggedly up and down. A straight line is certainly not necessary or even desirable when you're out for an afternoon's amble.

But, and make no mistake about it, going uphill and down are the most fun once you learn the techniques and "easy ways." (If you just want to go along on the flat, you might as well go ice skating, for heaven's sake!)

Nordic skiing differs from Alpine in that we need no motor-driven equipment to get us where we're going and no motor-driven lifts to get us to the top. We can easily climb any hill we come to, and, as you've seen, sliding down is really fun. And it can be tremendously exciting! That is what turns on our Alpine friends . . . understandably. One of the main reasons for frequent injuries in Alpine skiing, however, is that wait in a lift line—followed by a cold ride to the top. Then, suddenly, cold muscles, no warm-up, and a crazy rush down the hill!

Cross-country skiers are "warmed up" most of the time, and when we ski to the top of a hill, we already have a pretty good idea of the conditions that we'll experience coming back down.

But uphill, downhill, or flatlands—it's all skiing. As skill and confidence increase, you'll want to do more and more pure skiing. I can't remember a tour, ever, when we didn't stop and "do" a particular hill a few times . . . sometimes for hours!

Let's learn some turns, and then we'll practice all the uphill methods. Make your way back to the little hill of Hours 2 and 3. Make sure that you have a nice, skied surface, loosely packed and fairly smooth. If it has snowed since Hour 3, ski the hill a few times to break the surface. If it has been "sledded," try to rough it up a little with a few full-hill "screaming snowplows," or move to a slightly less slick hill. You are going to need a little traction until you get these moves grooved.

We turn for more than one reason. The first is obvious: so that you don't fetch up against that spruce or ski off the trail when it turns. The second reason for turning, when skiing on a nice "ski hill," is that it helps control your speed. The same reasons apply for turns in downhill skiing. The third reason, and just as important as the other two, is that turning is fun and feels good, especially when you realize that there are six or seven different ways to turn and that you can do them all on cross-country skis.

Some turns can be done easier than others, to be sure, but once we learn to harness these forces, we can execute some fairly sophisticated maneuvers and negotiate some pretty big hills. Lots of mountaineering is now done with our skinny skis, and there are even some ski patrollers using cross-country equipment up there. The reason is simple: they can manage the downhills and then easily climb back up.

Those patrollers are strong skiers, though. So we better make sure we know what we're doing before we attempt the headwall at our local hot hill!

HALF-SNOWPLOW TURNS. When you've got this mastered, you're going to feel like the European giant slalom champ. Listen to the following explanation. Then go back and listen to it again. Then look at the pictures, and finally go do it. To turn right:

1. Start downhill.
2. Go into a "medium" snowplow (18–24 inches between your feet). You're not trying to stop now. Just control your descent a little.
3. Drop your left shoulder down and back. (You'll actually be turning your upper body slightly *away* from the direction you wish to turn.)
4. Lean out over that left ski and . . . around to the right you'll go.

All we want for the first couple of turns (in both directions) is a deflection of a couple of degrees. Don't even try to "do 90s" yet! You'll see, though, that in your turn to the right, your left ski is doing most of the turning and that it is mostly sliding, just edging a tiny bit. Your right ski is just sort of hanging there. Later, as you get more powerful, you'll find that you're "pulling" a little against the uphill ski, that you're using the side of that ski (the right one in this case) to dig into the snow just a bit. It's premature to mention it now, but you'll see what I mean before the hour is over.

Now, this half-snowplow turn is kind of backward from anything that your brain "knows." You're turning your upper body *away* from the direction you want to turn, and your weight is downhill much of the time. In fact, you're actually leaning your upper body downhill. *Can this be right?* Yes! The concept might be hard to realize and understand, but it is very necessary.

Half-Snowplow Turn. Go into your snowplow position; shift your weight downhill out over the ski that's turned in the direction you want to go. Drop your downhill shoulder down and back. You're turning your upper body slightly away from the direction you want to turn; this helps your weighting. In the bottom pictures, I'm exaggerating, but it shows you the "shoulder down and back" idea. See how I weight the downhill ski and around I go.

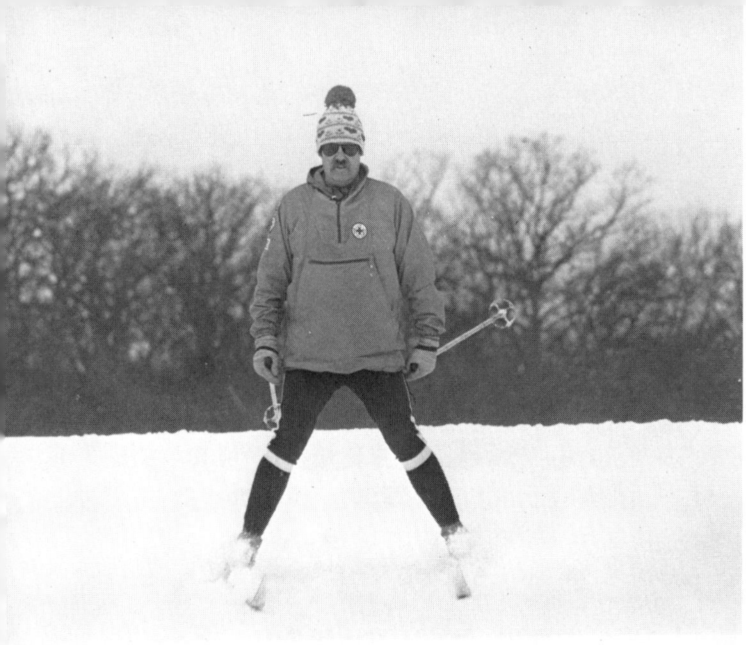
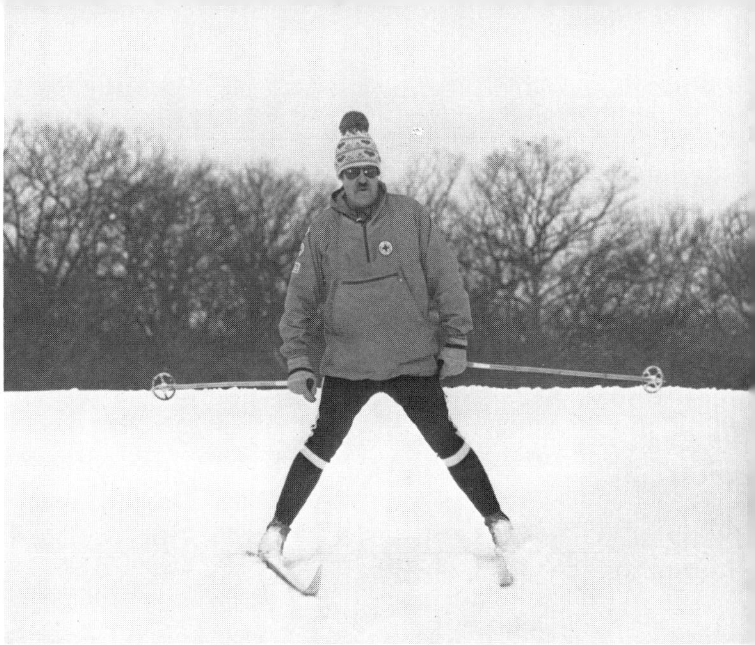
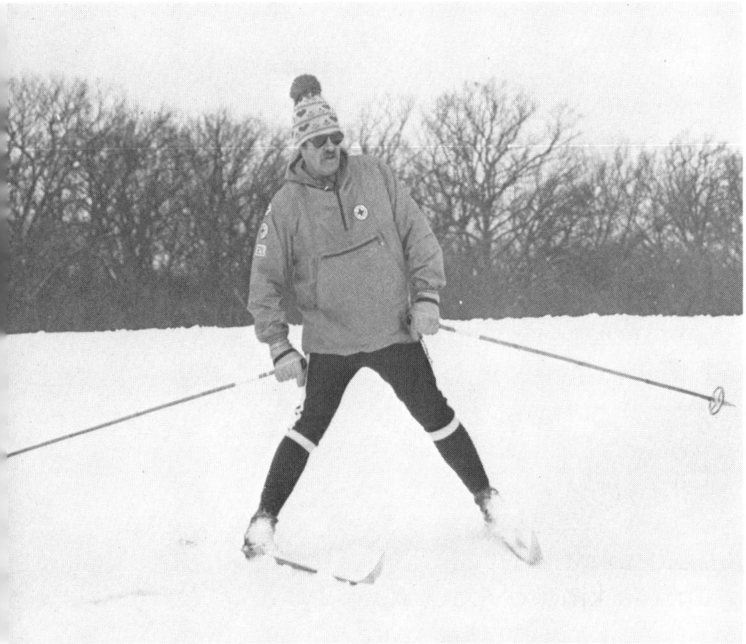
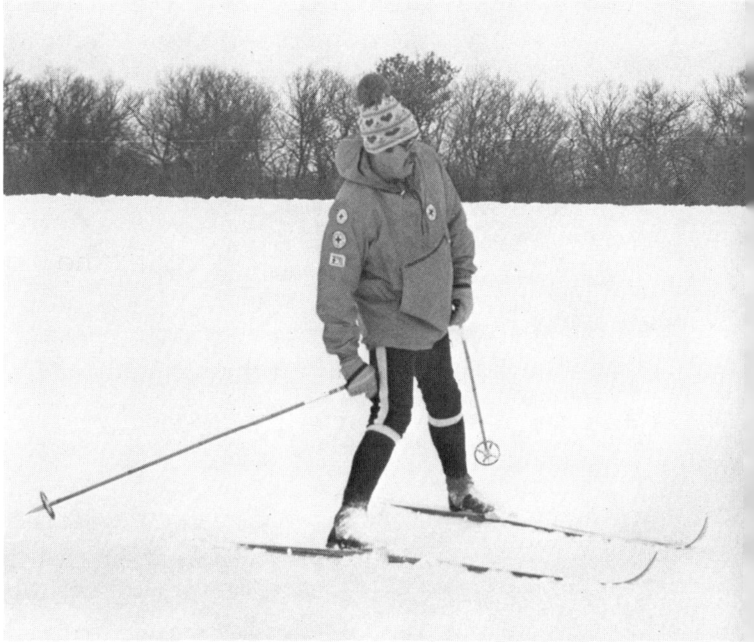
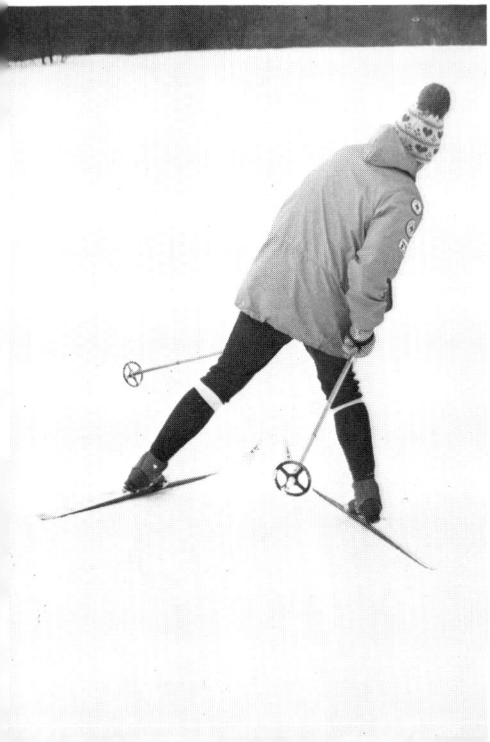
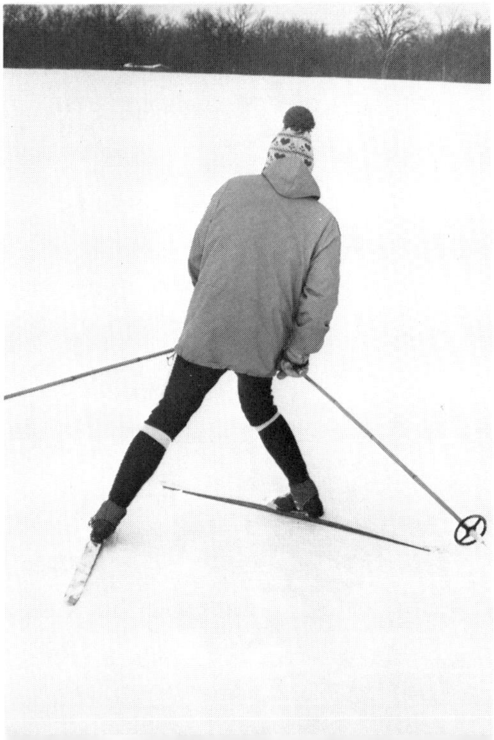
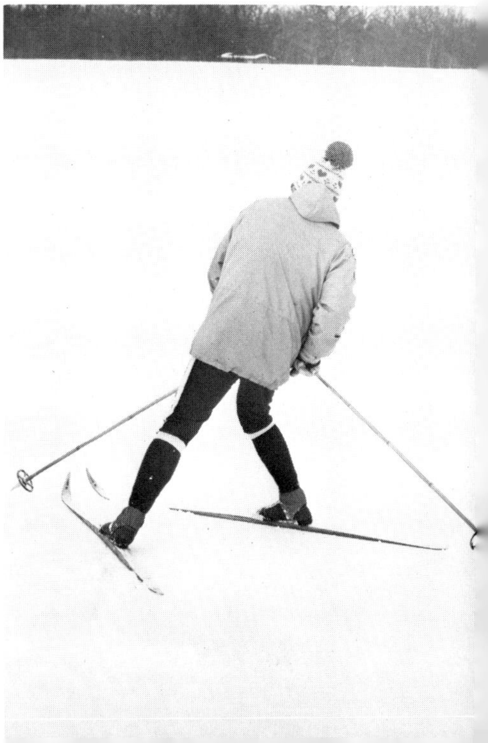

Let's take it from the top again. But first, park the poles! They're of little use here (except to help you get back uphill, and I'm sure you can manage without them on this little slope). Before we start down, go into your medium snowplow, just standing there looking at your skis. The right ski is heading left, and the left ski is heading right. In order to turn right, then, all you have to do is put more weight on the left ski.

Now let's start down again. We'll turn to the left this time. Take a couple of kicks to get up some speed. As soon as you're moving well, go into the snowplow position. Then drop your right shoulder down and pull it back. (It feels as though you're cocking your arm to throw a punch.) As soon as you "pull back," your weight transfers to your right ski; you're leaning out over it a bit—and you begin to turn left! Notice that it's easier without the poles. And notice, too, that you're not falling down backward (and bumping your head) anymore. You're concentrating on holding your body correctly, and you can't bend forward at the waist, overcompensate, and end up on your back!

If, at this point, you feel that "I can turn left, but I can't go right" or vice versa, don't give it another thought. Everybody has a "sweet side." You'll just have to concentrate a little more on the weak side and try to get comfortable with it. When we start linking these turns, begin with your weaker side, and then every other time, when your "good" side comes up, you'll get a little blast of confidence.

Now look at the pictures on page 76. Exaggerate your shoulder turning at first. Later, you won't need to turn your upper body so much, but it helps as you learn. Practice half-snowplow turns singly, in both directions. And try to manage turning more and more. Soon, you should be able to turn 90 degrees and end up skiing across the hill . . . and stopping. Without drama. That's the easy way to stop. In control.

Q. My skis are crossing and I'm crashing!
A. Then you're not holding your snowplow position aggressively enough! Get your skis in position and make them stay that way. Don't let them cross. You're the boss!

4. & 5.

Now, I think you're ready for a little exercise that will get you going both directions and show you how much you've learned about control and turning.

LINKED HALF-SNOWPLOW TURNS. Get your ski poles and plant them in the snow about 15 or 20 feet apart on the best part of the hill. Now return to the top. This time, we're going to slalom around the poles. (You can put up 2 or 3 pairs if you have them. It's even more fun. And you can time each other . . . have a real "Giant Slalom" race and pretend you're all in the Olympics.)

The idea is to go around all the poles alternately to "port" and "starboard." Start with a right turn, then execute a left turn, and so on. If you cut it too close, go back and set the pole up again and try once more. If you lose concentration, catch an edge, or ski off straight after an attempted turn, no matter. Just go back and try it again.

Stop! Let's learn one more thing about turning right now. On skis you're sliding and side-slipping when you do most of these turns. You can't just drive up to the corner, turn left, and drive away. You must anticipate your turn. You must have completed your turning motions before you reach the object you're trying to get around! When you slalom, you should already be in your right turn as you round the pole to your left, and so on. You should set up for the next turn before you pass the pole that you're going around!

After a few times down this slalom course (try starting on both sides of the first pole), you should be turning right and left with almost the same ease. You'll see that linking these half-snowplow turns is very graceful, that the transition from right to left is a "body float" rather than a "body slam," and that you must remain aggressive to do them well. But, by golly, you *can* do them.

Now pick up your poles and try one or two more half-snowplow turns with them on. They just go along for the ride at first, but after you've learned how to do the turns, your poles will add a little stability.

It's actually easier without your poles. They don't really do any work in this turn.

MOVING STEP TURNS. Now we're ready for another turn, a much easier one to learn and the most useful and most used turn in cross-country skiing: the moving step turn.

This turn isn't as graceful as the half-snowplow, but it has some real advantages. After you have invested all the kinetic energy necessary to climb a hill, you will want to get as much back as possible when you go down the other side. When you snowplow, you "spend" part of this stored energy scrubbing off speed with your plow. You won't waste anywhere near as much energy when you use the moving step turn.

Remember the first time we had to turn around on the flat, do a 180-degree "flower" and go back the way we came? We learned to turn using the standing step turn. I told you then that you needed to master the toe lift, heel down, press down on the tail of the ski "because we're going to need to know how later." This is "later." The moving step turn is the big brother of that little turnaround. It works as a series of little "scissors" down the hill, a little series of hops.

1. Start downhill.
2. Lean back, just a little.
3. Pull up with your toes on the inside of your boots, with your ankles held rigid.
4. Pivot one ski (either one) out a few inches, plant it, transfer weight to it, and quickly pivot the other ski around parallel to it. Lift the tip of each ski a couple of inches off the snow. Keep the tails down.
5. Rest a beat.
6. Pivot the first one again, and quickly "close it up." Step, step, pause; step, step, pause; and so forth.
7. Your poles can help you maintain your balance and might actually jab the snow from time to time. Of course, shift your weight from right to left each time (or vice versa).

When you begin, just try to get a few degrees of deviation—just two "hops" in either direction. As soon as your balance comes in, you can begin "stepping" farther around. Soon, you will be able to manage a full 90 degrees, and then

78

4. & 5.

Moving Step Turn. This is our most useful turn, the big brother of the standing step turn. Note in the bottom picture the arched foot in the upraised ski. The tail is still down hard on the snow. At first it is a series of hops . . . move one ski a foot, then "close it up."

you'll actually turn and turn until you're facing slightly back uphill . . . and you stop.

The moving step turn is the main trail turn and the one you'll use most often when you have to turn quickly—when the decision to turn must be made quickly and there's not enough time to set up for one of the more elaborate turns.

It's critical to remember to keep the tail of the ski that's being moved down *tight* on the snow. That provides stability and helps you keep your balance. If you want proof, you'll find that you can pick up the tip of one ski and, if you keep that ski's tail pressed down hard, ski all the way down the hill with a fair amount of stability.

See? The moving step turn was easier to master than the half-snowplow. And I think you'll recognize that they are completely different turns and should be used at different times and in different situations. The choice soon will become instinctive.

Let's link some moving step turns down to the bottom of the hill and then learn a flatland "power turn," the "skating turn." And since we'll be at the bottom, next we can learn our six ways uphill.

SKATING TURNS. Here is a cross-country racer's flatland turn that has an application in everyday touring. It's a trail turn "with the power on" and has many uses—the most important of which is (again) getting you out of trouble in a hurry! From time to time, if you are skiing aggressively, you will get into situations where you will need power and control to stay on the trail. Example: You're skiing in prepared tracks, slightly downhill. The trail takes a sharp turn (either way), and the groomed trail disappears completely in the turn area itself (a frequent occurrence). Trees lie dead ahead of you and you're *moving*. Solutions: Bail out (boo) or make a fast skating turn (correct). That's what I mean by trouble, and you can handle it!

Skating Turn. I'm pushing off with my left ski, weight on my right.

Let's try turning to the right first. Starting on the flat and pushing off from your left ski, lift your right ski off the snow. (This is about the only time you'll ever do this.) Turn your in-the-air right ski out about 20 or 30 degrees (maybe 1½ or 2 feet) and "skate out" with it. Shift your weight to this ski. Actually push against your left ski and "jump" to the right one. The maneuver resembles the way you turn on ice skates.

Push yourself strongly in the new direction with your left pole. The right pole acts as a stabilizer, and as soon as your weight is all on the right ski and you are gliding, pick up your left ski and swing it around parallel to the right one. Now you're ready for your next "skate." Rest a beat and repeat the process. When you're doing skating turns in a tight circle, you'll feel as though you are falling to the right and catching yourself with the right ski as it skates out.

Turns to the left are exactly the same (except the procedure is reversed). Cut a couple of "figure 8s," noticing that you actually can get up a pretty good head of steam. Notice, too, how tired you are after a couple of these "8s." The skating turn takes a lot of energy, and that's why we'll not be using it too much as we tour. But when we need it, it's there.

UPHILL SIX WAYS. And now . . . maybe after a little sip of your water and a tumble onto the snow for a 45-second rest . . . we're ready to learn the six ways uphill. We have been doing the first, the straight uphill, but let's review it and then go on to the other five.

It's going to take you about 10 minutes to learn these six ways, and after you have learned them, you'll not have to think too much about them. You'll automatically start with the easiest, shift to the next slower (but surer), and so forth, until you find the technique that will get you up the hill.

After we've gone uphill using the various methods, try your half-snowplow or moving step turns coming back down. Practice each of the six ways at least one full climb of the hill. The straight uphill should be practiced enough so that you really begin to enjoy it. (I'm not kidding!)

The six ways uphill are:

1. The straight uphill.
2. The uphill traverse.
3. The straight sidestep.
4. The sidestep traverse.
5. The herringbone.
6. The IAEF method.

The Straight Uphill. Straight uphill running is the easiest of the six (if you're waxed correctly or, especially, if you are on no-wax skis) and the one that gives me the most pleasure when I roar over the top of a hill.

Standing flat-footed on your skis, put just a little more spring in your knees and lean back! Yes, you want to weight your heels. Now, with short, quick slides, move off the flat and start uphill. As you start up, get your arms and poles way back behind

82

The First Method: Straight Uphill. Notice that I'm leaning slightly back, weighting my heels. With poles way out back, take short little shuffles and look uphill!

4. & 5.

you, out of sight behind your back. Look up, over the crest of the hill, if it's not too high. This is still "diagonal striding," so your left pole and right ski will move at the same time. Holding your poles way back there will keep you from sliding back and will provide some of the "drive" uphill. When it is all coming together, your arms/poles will be acting like pistons, driving back into the snow as you slide, slide, slide uphill.

As you near the crest and the hill starts to level off, lengthen your stride, slow your tempo, and just glide away in your usual cross-country kick. Most "uncoached" skiers (and even some experienced ones who should know better) want to lean forward as they go uphill. That is exactly *wrong*. Leaning forward moves your weight toward the tips of your skis and defeats what you are trying to do. When you correctly lean back, you move your weight toward the tails and help the skis resist slipping backward.

The Uphill Traverse. What if the hill is too steep to straight uphill run? Then we shift to No. 2: the uphill traverse. Instead of heading straight up the fall line, on this steeper hill we're going to start up across the hill (traversing) and, in effect, reduce the steepness of the angle. Naturally, you will try to go up at as sharp an angle as you can, comfortably, to reduce the number of times you will have to "tack."

After you have gone up 10 or 15 slides (poles back and working, of course), come to a stop while still angled uphill, do a kick turn (uphill ski first), go up 10 or 15 more strides, kick turn again, and so on. The result is a zigzag route uphill, similar to tacking a sailboat into the wind.

The width of the trail sometimes will limit your ability to get this technique working effectively. So we will need another "plan" for a steep uphill ascent.

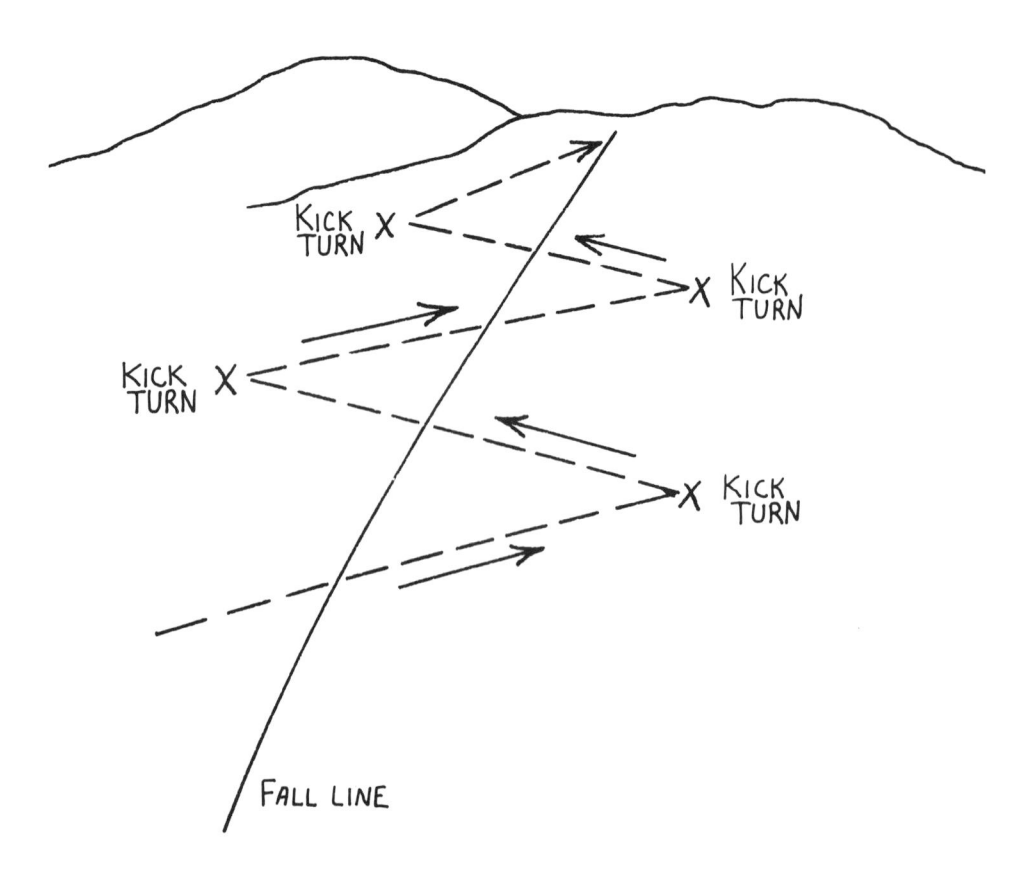

The Second Method: Uphill Traverse. "Tacking" uphill with a kick turn at every direction change.

The Straight Sidestep. Straight sidestepping is a most effective method. It will get you up inclines that are nearly vertical. You will use it on every tour, up a stream bed (or down), through a ditch, over a fallen tree. It is dead slow but very sure . . . and all it requires is pickin' 'em up and layin' 'em down.

Standing sideways and edging your skis *into* the hill, step sideways uphill 1 foot or 18 inches; then close it up and step up again. It is just the same and just as positive as climbing stairs sideways, one step at a time.

Going downhill is just the same, including edging your skis uphill, into the hill. What you are doing, of course, is making a little series of stair steps. Your poles merely provide balance and stability. They don't work much.

4.&5.

The Third Method: Straight Sidestep. Just "walking up stairs sideways." Pick them up and move up (or down). It will get you up just about anything. The Fourth Method: Sidestep Traverse. Moving ahead and up with kick turns at every direction change.

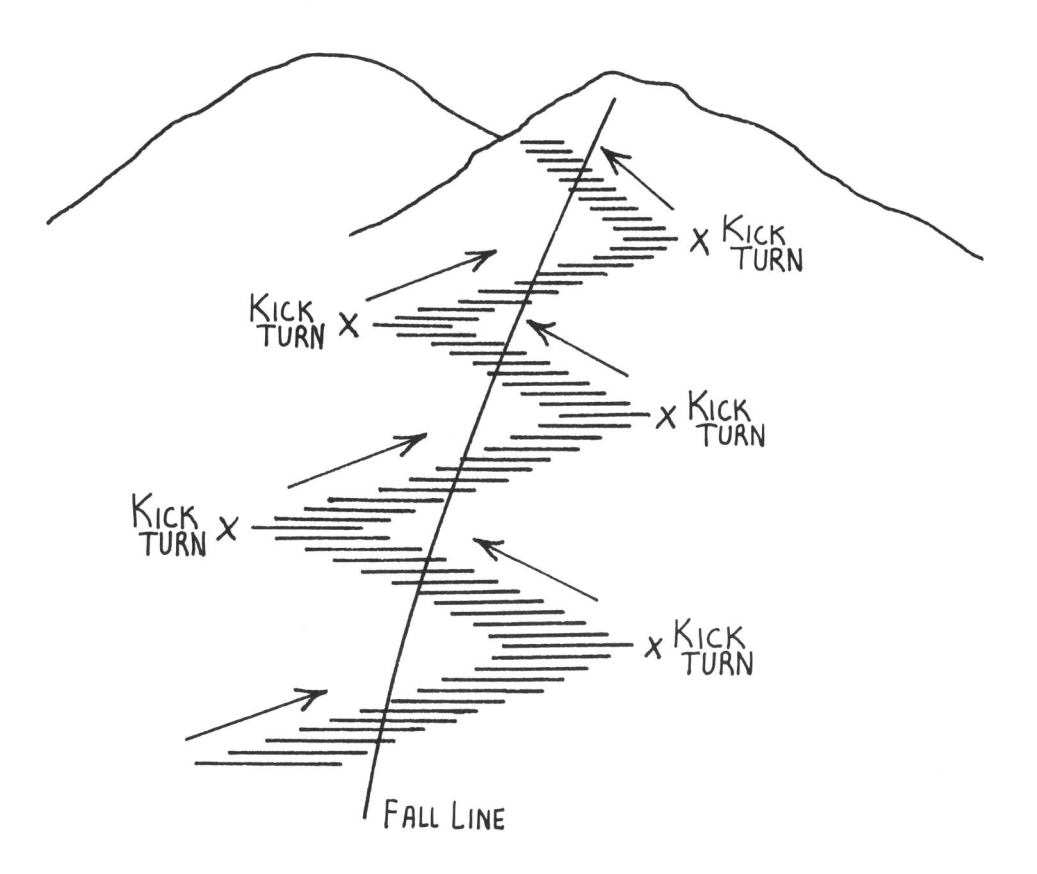

85

The Sidestep Traverse. An alternate sidestep, about as sure and a little faster, is the sidestep traverse. It works this way. Standing sideways to the hill, shoulder uphill, step up and *forward* with your uphill ski. Walk that ski 1 foot or 18 inches up the hill and forward about 2 feet at the same time. Close it up, and do it again. When you have done 10 or 15 steps, or when you run out of trail, do a kick turn (always uphill first) and continue stepping up and forward and closing it up. It is not really fast, but it will get the job done. The sidestep traverse is a good "change-up" to use on very long climbs. You are able to go slow enough to get some rest.

The Herringbone. Conversely, the herringbone is the fastest way up any given hill—and the most energy intensive. It is a lot of work, but it's what Nordic racers usually use to get over the hill

The Fifth Method: Herringbone. The tracks look like a fish skeleton. Use reverse edging, with poles moving fast. This is best if done quickly, at a run.

in a hurry. The technique is called the herringbone because the tracks you leave in your uphill climb look like a fish skeleton.

The herringbone is similar in many ways to the straight uphill. Lean back, poles and arms behind you, and splay out your skis in a "V" pattern, exactly opposite the pattern of the snowplow. Keep your ski tips wide apart, allowing the tails to form the point of the "V." With our long skis, we have to lift each tail pretty high to "step over" the other and avoid coming down on the back of the opposite ski.

I used to find the herringbone hard to do and avoided it, other than showing my classes how to do it. One day, I realized that if most racers use it most of the time, it must not be *that* hard to do. So I stopped hating it. Suddenly, it all came together for me when I radically increased my tempo! In order to make the herringbone work on cross-country skis, you have to attack the hill. Run and kick your legs far enough apart so that you don't step on your own skis. Remember, you are leaning back, your arms and poles are way back (pumping like pistons into the snow), and you are bending your ankles in, edging your skis to keep them biting. That's why the herringbone is fast—you more or less "get up on top" of the snow and keep going. When it comes together for you, you will know what I mean.

Yes, the herringbone can be done slowly, but you sink down and bog down so much that it's very slow, much work, no fun, and *not worth it*. Learn to do it fast, and you will learn to enjoy it as I have. (*Tip:* Have a race with yourself to the top.)

The IAEF Method. And that leaves only the IAEF method. To the best of my knowledge, I'm the only instructor teaching this most useful technique. Oh, I didn't invent it. Everybody has done it occasionally; but hardly anyone has come to terms with it, recognized it as a legitimate uphill method. Once a skier gets the boards on, he or she is terribly reluctant to take them off. Even though removing skis has become easier and easier with the newer bindings, there is something in human nature that says, "If I take 'em off, I'm a quitter." It's a macho hangup (for men *and* women).

The Sixth Method: IAEF (If All Else Fails).

Well, that's wrong! There are objects that you just can't get up over, down, or around with your skis on. You probably could climb a flight of stairs in your house with your 205s on—in a half-hour or so. But why would you want to? The same logic applies to that ice-covered stream bank, the big fallen tree, the very narrow, very steep trail, and so forth. Recognize the IAEF method! I give you permission to use it . . . wisely. But *do* use it where it will save you time, energy, and bruised knees. IAEF means "If All Else Fails." The technique is simple: reach down and unfasten the bale catches on your bindings, step out, reach down, pick up your skis—and walk up (or down) the hill. Show me where it says on your skis, "You can't take these off."

4. & 5.

One last thought on this subject before we move on to Hour 6 and, finally, learn how to *cross-country ski*. You will come to downhill trails in your touring that you can't solve. Your mind will say, "I'm scared to do that because it's icy and there's a big tree dead ahead and I don't know how to negotiate this part of the trail on skis." And another voice will say, "Go ahead, you big baby . . . just push off and do it."

IAEF it. Take your skis off, step out of the tracks, off to one side, and walk down to the point where you're comfortable again. What would you prove if you fetched up against that oak or broke a ski and had to walk all the way back?

Use your head. If it's beyond your skill level, don't fight it. Remember, *every* cross-country skier comes across a trail section somewhere that is beyond his skill level. (Yours is just waiting for you out there!) The brave and lucky skiers make it; the others crash. It's good for you to say, "Okay, trail, you win, you're too tough for me" once in a while. Even Muhammad Ali lost!

Hours 4.&5.   Timecheck

- ☐ Hill Prep
- ☐ Half-Snowplow Turns: 1 Hour
    - ☐ Right: 15 Minutes
    - ☐ Left: 15 Minutes
    - ☐ Linked: 10 Minutes
    - ☐ Slalom: 20 Minutes
- ☐ Moving Step Turns: 20 Minutes
    - ☐ Right: 8 Minutes
    - ☐ Left: 8 Minutes
    - ☐ Linked: 4 Minutes
- ☐ Skating Turns: 10 Minutes
    - ☐ Figure 8s: 5 Minutes
- ☐ Uphill Methods: 25 Minutes
    - ☐ Straight Uphill: 10 Minutes
    - ☐ Uphill Traverse: 2 Minutes
    - ☐ Straight Sidestep: 3 Minutes
    - ☐ Sidestep Traverse: 3 Minutes
    - ☐ Herringbone: 5 Minutes
    - ☐ IAEF: 2 Minutes

Hour 6.

✶ DIAGONAL STRIDE

✶ POLE USE

✶ EXPERT KICK

✶ DOUBLE POLING

✶ BREATHING

✶ UPHILL RUNNING

Hour 6.

HOW TO CROSS-COUNTRY SKI

✸

BY NOW, YOU CAN GET ALONG ON THE FLAT, STOP, GO UPHILL AND DOWN, AND DO SOME TURNS. IT'S ABOUT TIME THAT WE PUT IT ALL TOGETHER . . . AND THAT YOU *LEARN HOW TO CROSS-COUNTRY SKI!* THIS WILL BE A HARD HOUR. (NONE OF THEM HAVE BEEN EASY, HAVE THEY? CAN YOU IMAGINE, IN THE ACTUAL SCHOOL WE DO THIS ALL IN ONE DAY . . . FROM 10:30 A.M. TO 4:30 P.M.)

Back to the flat for this last hour. If your earlier tracks still exist, fine. If not, make them again. Carve out a set of straight, level tracks about 100 yards long. Ski it twice to get it nice and packed, and then stop at the end and park your poles one last time.

This hour will include a couple of hard exercises, plus some help to get everything working. Please *do* these exercises. Don't cheat yourself and skip ahead or think, "I'll do them later." We are going to work on our diagonal stride (haven't mentioned that much before, yet it's the basis of all touring), the proper use of the poles in the diagonal stride, the expert kick, double poling, breathing correctly, and (once again) uphill running.

DIAGONAL STRIDE. The diagonal stride requires legs, arms, kick, glide, and push all to work together easily and rhythmically to cover great distances in an easy lope. It is the basic cross-country motion, where you put your head up, smile, pull off your gloves, open your wind shirt, and just "float" for miles. We're already doing everything right. Right ski/left pole, left ski/right pole, etc. All we have to learn is how to achieve more power and keep our glide going longer.

The Snowshoe Hop. The first exercise is the "snowshoe hop," and it will find you radically shifting your weight from ski to ski, pushing off against the trailing ski, and extending your glide. What we are after is a power kick and as much glide each time as possible. This glide at the end of each kick is "free" motion. The longer the glide, the easier our touring will be.

Start down your track by actually jumping from your stopped ski to the moving one; then glide. Now hop to the other ski and coast. We are going to make two round trips, four laps total, doing this curious little jump. As we do it, we will move our upper

Diagonal Stride. Here is my easy, ground-covering lope. Note that the left pole plants opposite the right foot. When you get the trailing ski into the air at the end of your kick, you're getting a "bang."

Snowshoe Hop. I'm hopping from one ski to the other and my weight is shifting way out over the gliding ski.

body from side to side, as much as one foot in either direction. Your weight will transfer out over each coasting ski as you jump from the planted one. It should feel as though the stationary ski were a snowshoe, absolutely stuck in the snow and unable to push back.

Notice that you are getting a weight transfer along with the jump forward. The upper body movement from side to side accentuates the transfer. After you learn to control the weight transfer, you will be able to discontinue the side-to-side body motion.

You actually are learning how to kick with the "snowshoe" back ski. By the fourth and final lap it should be: (1) kick, a spring forward from the snowshoe ski; (2) complete weight transfer onto the coasting ski, accompanied by a body shift out over the coasting ski; (3) a gradual closing up of the back ski, actually pulling it along forward after the completion of the kick until that ski comes abreast of the coasting ski; and (4) as the back ski catches up and passes the former coasting ski, a weight shift to the new lead ski. Finally, repeat your kick/jump ahead from the new trailing ski.

This is a long explanation of what is basically the diagonal stride, with accentuated (and strengthened) leg motions. Take your time between hops . . . concentrate on power and glide. At the end of your four trips, you will be getting more glide than you would have imagined possible. You'll feel yourself getting stronger, too.

The Skateboard. Now, we are going to do four more laps (twice up and back) using the next strengthening exercise. This is a toughie, but it pays off in big dividends. You will want to do this one every week or so just to get that feel back. It's called the "skateboard," and it is done by putting both hands on one knee, holding that leg rigid (not moving it at all), and pushing yourself (and your rigid ski) along with the back ski (see photos).

You are sliding and gripping with the back ski. You will feel that it takes a great deal of finesse, a very sensitive touch to get it to grip and not slip back. You will feel almost as though you are curling your toes and digging in with them. Push yourself the whole length of your track with one ski, then turn, switch hands

Skateboard Exercise. The back ski is doing all the grabbing and pushing; the front ski is getting a free ride. It is the "skateboard."

Here's another view of the "skateboard."

(to the other knee), and push yourself back with the opposite leg. Don't cheat! I know it's hard, but do it and just wait! You can't imagine the magic that these two exercises will work.

Get your poles and rest while I tell you what part your poles will play in developing your "kick and bang." When we put kick, glide, push, and extend all together, we will be doing the picture-book diagonal stride.

POLE USE. Plant each of your poles just about even with the opposite foot (right pole plants opposite the left foot and vice versa) and *gently* push backward with them until they are quite a distance behind you. Next, push *hard* until your elbows lock and give your wrists and the poles a little "flip." This is the area where the poles really do their work—the last foot or so, as you ski away from one of the planted poles. (That's the reason for the downward bend of the pole tip: so it doesn't slip out when it is way back there pushing.)

A hard push will give you two feet or more of extra glide, more "free" motion. Now your legs/skis and arms/poles are working as a team, really covering ground. Your hands won't be able to hold the poles way back there. The straps will do all the work. Each back hand will be entirely off the grip, and your fingers will be extended.

As you glide forward, your momentum will pull your pole out of the snow, but you should hold it back there for just another fraction of a second . . . for a little "follow-through." Then flip the pole forward and plant it again opposite your foot.

EXPERT KICK. Got it? That is what your poles do. Let's ski up and down the track a few more times . . . smoothly, powerfully, rhythmically, and a little more aggressively. Get lots of glide. Look up. Knees are just slightly bent, actually just "unlocked." Lean into it a little . . . great! Feel the power? It should all be working.

When you're really moving, your pole will extend so far out behind you that you won't be able to hold onto the pole handle and the strap will do all the work.

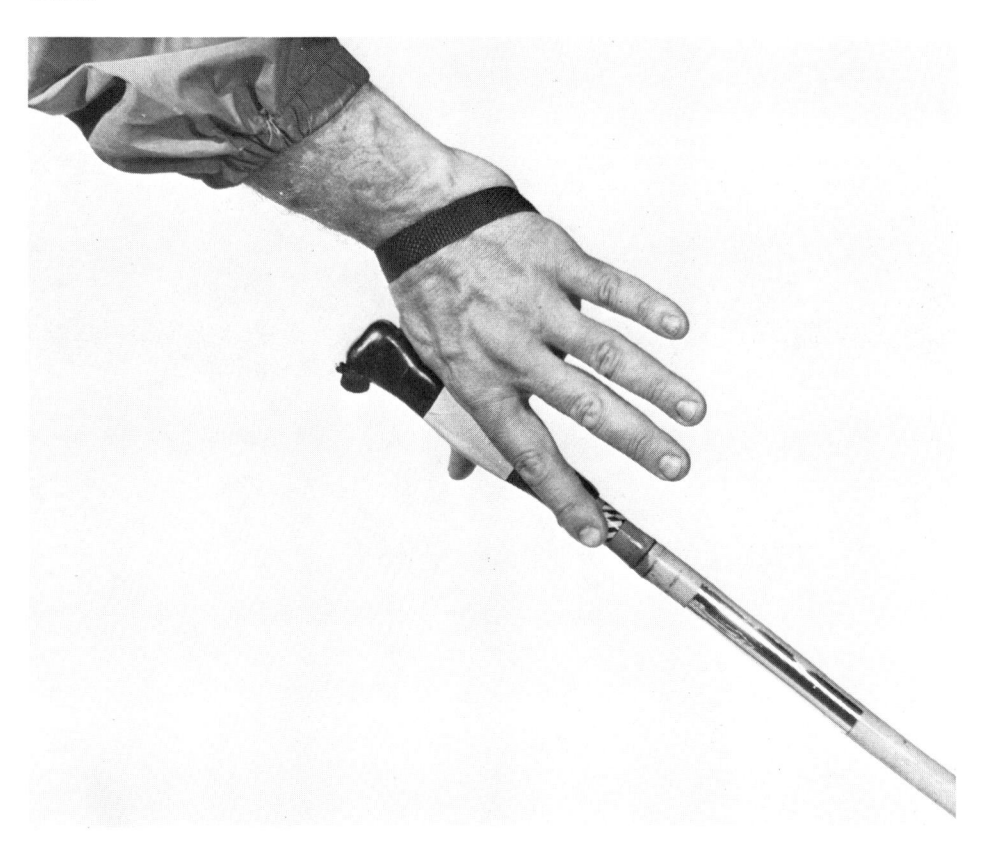

The second or third time down the track, when you were whistling, did your trailing ski tail come up off the snow? Good! You've got it! That is the ultimate follow-through of your kick, frequently referred to as the "bang." When you can consistently get that tail up 1 foot or 18 inches, you are *cross-country skiing*. The ski tips will stay in the tracks (you haven't had those tracking problems for the last couple of hours, have you?). Bindings are mounted so that the ski is just ever so slightly heavier in the front—to help them keep tracking. (Lift up a ski by the unsnapped bale and watch it hang down a little . . . unbalanced.)

Your "professional" diagonal stride will take you endless, effortless miles. The more you do it correctly, the stronger you'll get—and the smoother. You will feel the little bobbing motion as you get into it. Notice, too, that you now are getting the weight transfer without the side motion.

Expert Kick. Note the trailing ski coming off the snow. Now you've really got your skis moving.

Double Poling. Arms, shoulders, and poles doing all the work.

DOUBLE POLING. For a change of pace (to rest), let's learn one more little "racer's trick." It is called "double poling," and it is used as a breather on the trail. It is done mostly with your arms, shoulders, and upper body while your legs "rest." But it also can be used with an occasional single kick. Here are two ways.

Moving along the trail in your diagonal stride, you decide to "rest" by double poling for 50 feet. Produce an extra good kick to get a long glide going, and bring both skis up parallel in your "downhill" position. Plant both poles about even with your feet and, sinking down rapidly, pull hard on your poles and squirt your skis ahead for a long, fast glide. As you begin to slow down, plant those poles and hang on them again. The sinking movement augments the power in your arms and lets you double pole with less effort. This is hard work for your upper body but good exercise.

Here is the racer's way to do "sinking" double poling. Just as your arms/poles are fully extended, kick with one leg to get even more glide. Then bring your skis up together again, double pole, extend, and kick with the other leg . . . and so on. It is a much different pace. A nice little mental and physical change-up.

Here's another view of double poling. Note hands way out in back.

BREATHING. Let's work on breathing for a minute. I'm going to teach you how cross-country racers breathe. Tourers can do the same and be much less winded at the end of a fast mile stretch. We are going to breathe *out*, forcefully, emptying the lungs of most of their air and not worrying about breathing in at all—it will happen all by itself.

   Here is the pattern. After you start your rhythmic diagonal stride, begin your forceful exhalations on a regular basis, for example, every time you extend your left pole. You should sound like an old steam engine as you go along. I call it "chuffing." You should be making a sound like "whoosh," "whoosh." Try it. Breathing this way, you should be able to stop at the end of your hard-skied mile and still be able to carry on a fairly normal conversation.

UPHILL RUNNING. Now for one last skill to end this hour: uphill running. We talked about it during our discussion of six ways uphill in Hours 4 & 5, but I did not go into the theory—or share the fun. Yes, it really is fun! The idea is to set a tempo goal for the hill, something you can live with, and go all the way to the top, using this tempo.

Diagonal stride to the base of the hill, bend your knees a little more, lean back, keep your poles back, and shorten your stride down to a fast shuffle. Keep trying to get some glide, even a few inches. Look up over the crest of the hill—and go up!

If you run uphill aggressively, you will get a tremendous lift as you near the top. As the hill begins to level off, you will find that your stride will automatically stretch out again. Your glide will lengthen, and you will be over the top! It will seem as though the hill hardly slowed you down. What a feeling!

And that just about concludes the six hours. You now have been exposed to all the basics of cross-country skiing. You now know how to do everything you will need for a lifetime of happy cross-country fun.

The best thing about learning it all at once is that with each outing, every tour or short amble, you will improve—for as long as you ski! I learn something or get a little better feeling about something *every time out*. (And I've been cross-country skiing for nine years.) This is an activity that you can enjoy with only minimum proficiency . . . and every day out you will get more proficient and enjoy it more.

What follows is an additional "hour," with some instruction on advanced turns and other interesting "extras." In my one-day course this comes at the end of the "school." It is an extra hour, and it is optional. I find that those students who really "got it" usually stay, and the ones who need more practice are frequently too tired to remain.

If you are trying to master cross-country skiing, I suggest that you consider resting at least overnight before tackling this "extra hour." The better you are at the skills learned in the first six hours, the more you will enjoy the "extras" of Hour 7.

Hour 6. Timecheck

- [ ] Snowshoe Hop Exercise: 12 Minutes
    - [ ] Four Trips
- [ ] Skateboard Exercise: 12 Minutes
    - [ ] Four Trips
- [ ] Pole Extend: 5 Minutes
- [ ] Complete Diagonal Stride with Expert Kick: 15 Minutes
    - [ ] Four Trips
- [ ] Double Poling: 5 Minutes
    - [ ] Arms Only
    - [ ] With Single Kick
- [ ] "New Breathing": 3 Minutes
- [ ] Uphill Running: 8 Minutes

Hour 7.

✶ "HELICOPTER" TURNS

✶ SNOWPLOW CHRISTIES

✶ HOCKEY STOPS

✶ PARALLEL TURNS

✶ TELEMARK TURNS

Hour 7.

"BIG KID STUFF"

✳

BEFORE WE GET INTO THESE ADVANCED TURNS, LET ME THROW IN A DISCLAIMER OF SORTS. THERE ARE MANY MORE KINDS OF ADVANCED TURNS THAN WE ARE GOING TO COVER. WE WILL LEARN THE SNOWPLOW CHRISTIE (OR BEGINNING CHRISTIE); THE HOCKEY STOP; THE BASIC PARALLEL TURN (IN THIS CASE, SORT OF A "HALF-HOCKEY STOP" TURN); AND THE FAMOUS TELEMARK TURN. THERE ARE MANY MORE TURN VARIATIONS POSSIBLE ON CROSS-COUNTRY SKIS, EVEN WITHOUT HAVING THE HEELS TIED DOWN (EXCEPT BY GRAVITY).

If you still want to "play" more after you've finished this hour, get one of the many good downhill technique books and learn all the christies (down-stem, up-stem, and so forth), the arlbergs, wedeln, garlands, and carved turns. If you find a real good one, let me know. I haven't even *tried* them all yet, and one of the things I love about cross-country is that I am always learning something new.

I frequently hear downhillers, inexperienced on cross-country equipment, say: "You can't edge on cross-country skis." Hogwash!

Without the ability to edge to some degree, you would have very limited control. One of the reasons for the narrower widths (52 to 55 mm) of the new, light touring equipment is the ease of "rolling" the skis up onto their edges to provide bite. Oh, how I love to *agree* with these "experts," then ski away, do a fast hockey stop, and come back to ask them to repeat their statement! I guess that is a little "show-offey," but by the middle of this seventh hour, you will be "hockey stopping" too. And it's really fun to show your stuff sometimes!

"HELICOPTER" TURNS.   Here's a little turn that you absolutely have no need for. I saw two people doing it at a touring resort a couple of years ago and found out that they learned it in Europe. It is so flashy that you might as well learn it . . . and who knows? There just might come a time when you will need it. There's a trick here, too, that enables one to do it easily.

The "helicopter" is an aerial 180-degree turn done on the flat. Say you want to turn around and ski right back in the tracks

Helicopter Turn. First, I set myself. Then I bend my knees, ready to spring into the air.

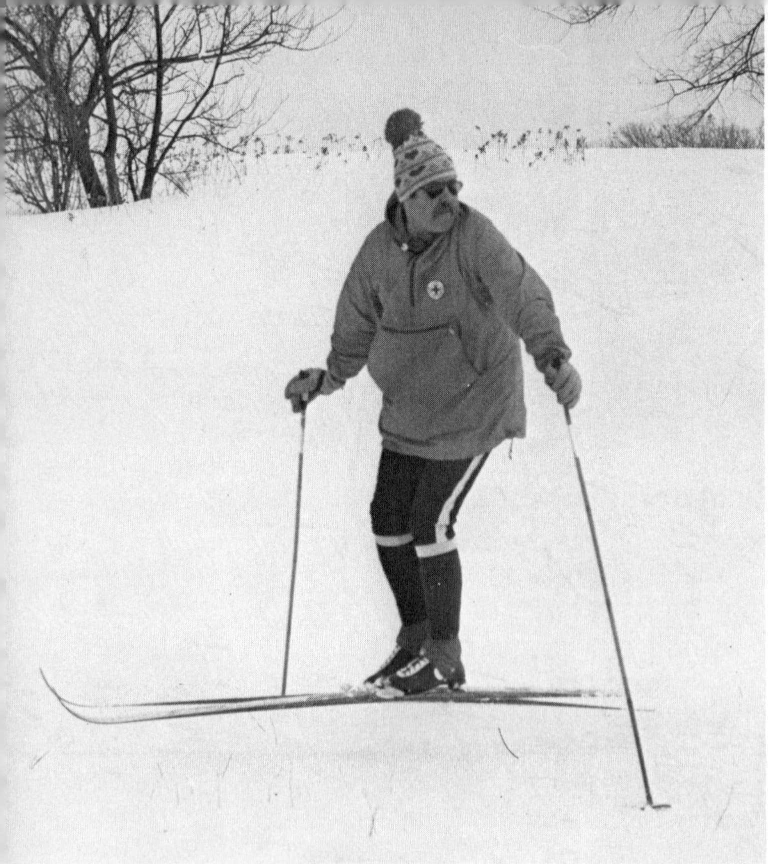
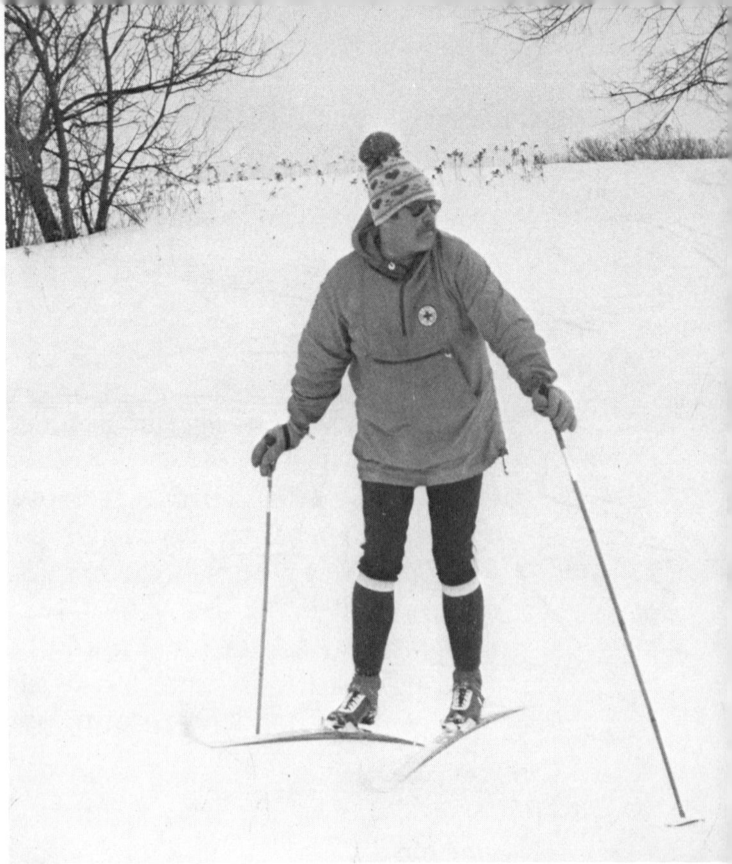
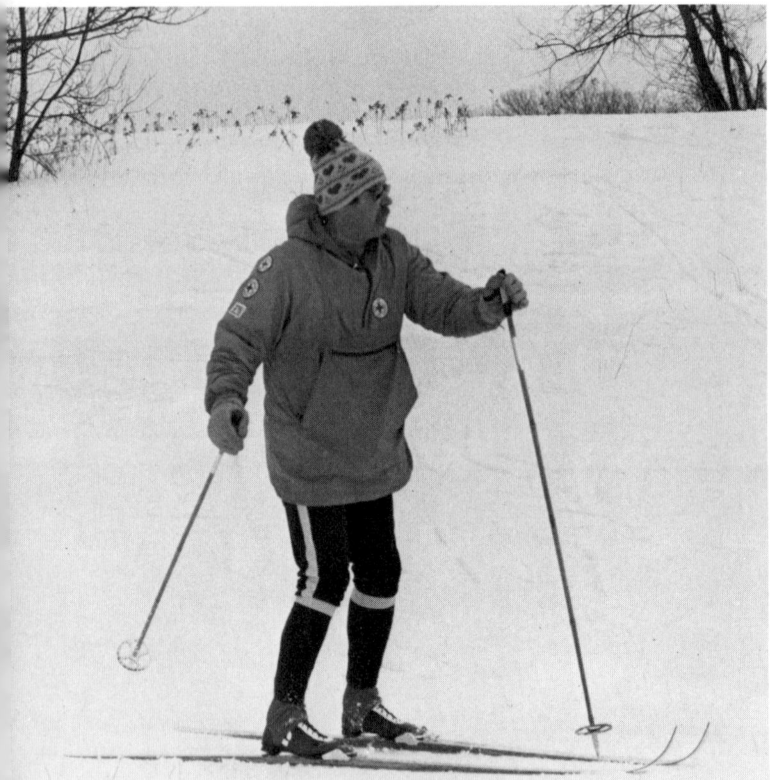
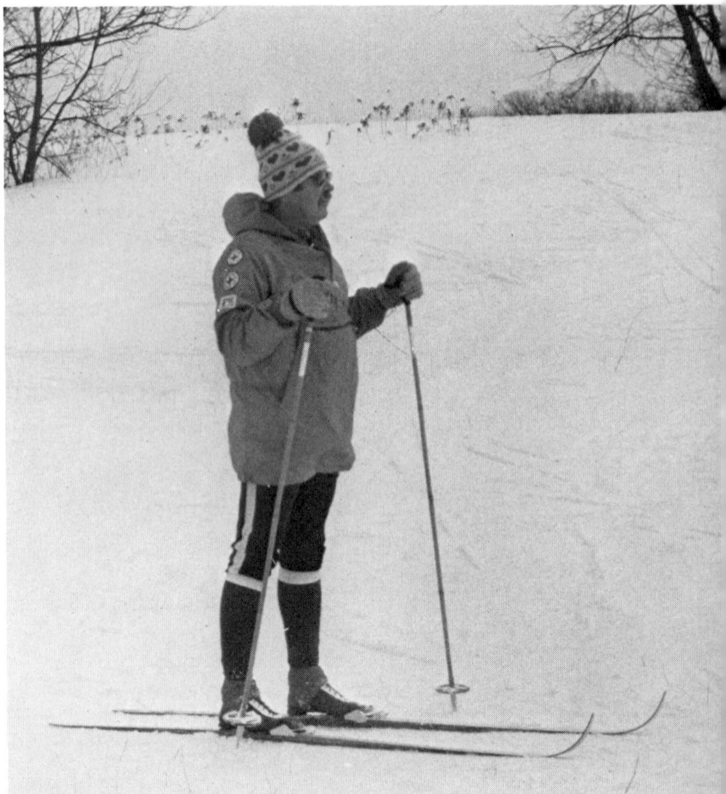

Helicopter Turn (cont.). I jump in the air, turning the skis. Notice the strain on the right pole. As I come around, the left pole lifts as the skis pass under it. This is the really quick 180 . . . try it.

you just arrived in. Try this. First, turn your upper body and head around and pick a "target." Any easily spottable object, such as a tree, that you want to be facing when you complete your turn will do. Then position your poles out of the swing range of your skis. (Look at the pictures.) For a helicopter to the left, the left pole is held behind you and out about 18 inches to 2 feet. The basket should be behind your left ski tail. The right pole is forward and out about 1 foot to 18 inches, not quite as far forward as the left one is back.

Got your target in mind? Now sink down and jump into the air. (Use your arms and poles to help, too.) As your skis come up off the snow, throw your upper body and head around until they're facing your target. (*The trick:* your legs and skis will follow.) Your right pole will pick up and follow you around, too, and your ski tips should have no trouble in missing your left pole as they come around.

That's it. You should be able to do it in either direction. The key is the target. You will have trouble turning far enough unless you know where you're going. The "helicopter" doesn't work too well, by the way, in deep snow; your skis won't get very far off the ground. They are likely to catch if the snow is more than six inches deep.

SNOWPLOW, OR BEGINNING STEM, CHRISTIES. I considered sharing this with you when we were doing our half-snowplow turns but decided to wait until after the regular class. This is an easy transition from half-snowplows and a natural one. The "christie" (short for Christiana, the former name of Oslo, where the turn was developed) is the sideslipped movement as the skis come around parallel at the end of the turn. Christies will give you some real power at the end of your snowplow turns and get you ready for the wonderful world of downhill.

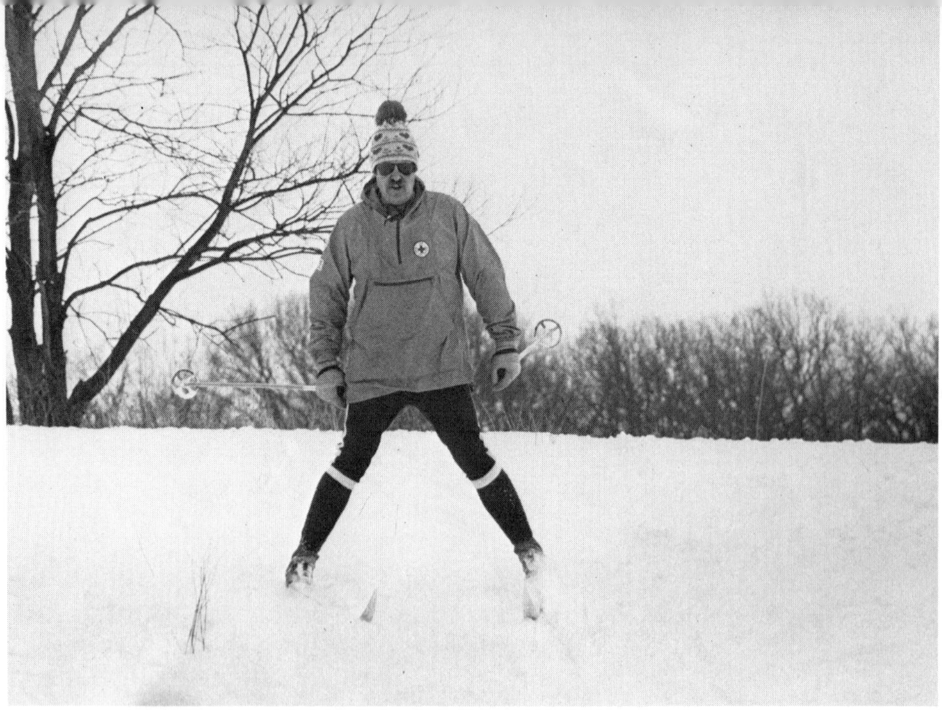

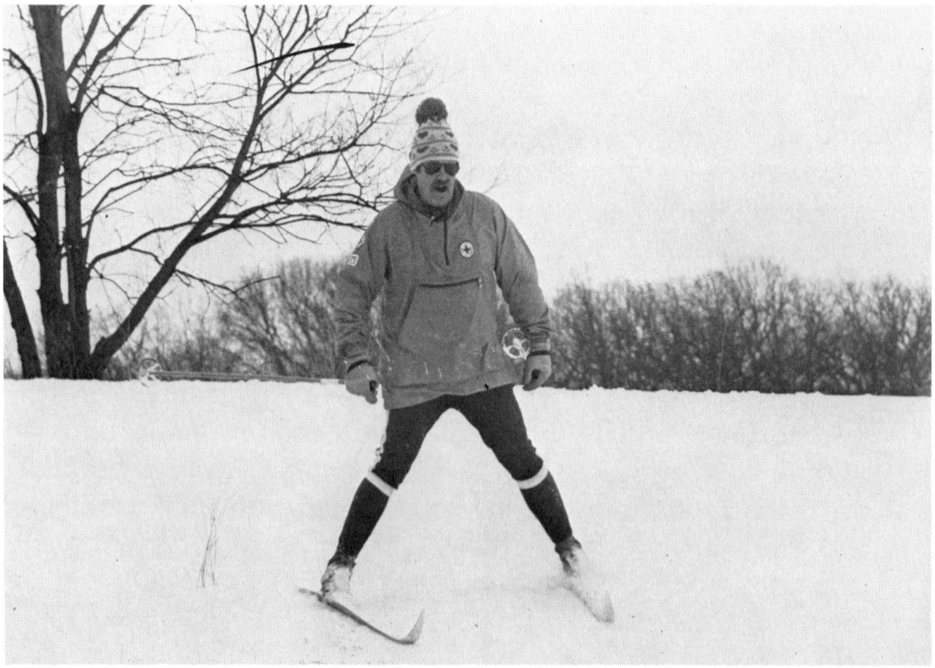

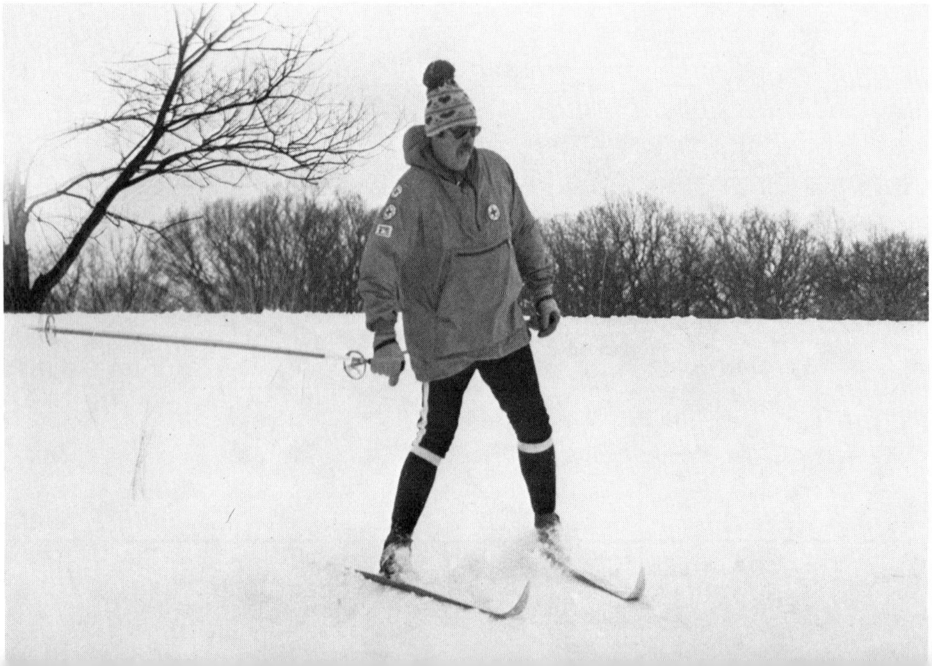

Snowplow Christie. It starts like the regular snowplow turn. When your weight is fully transferred to the downhill ski (bottom left), just pull the uphill ski around parallel to the turning ski and partially redistribute your weight over your skis.

Start downhill. Go into your half-snowplow position, one shoulder down and back, and as you begin to turn—as that downhill ski starts to slip—throw all of your weight on it. Keep it slipping sideways and turning. As soon as you are stable, slide your now unweighted uphill ski around parallel to the "working" ski, and slightly re-weight the now-slipping upper ski. Your skis are now side by side again, and as you round out the turn and stop, you will get an idea of how much fun parallel turns can be.

You can, of course, link snowplow christies by going into the snowplow again, starting your turn in the other direction, and, as you break loose, christie them around parallel. The reason for using the snowplow at the beginning of the christie is to start your side-slip, that is, break your skis loose and start them side-slipping so you can pull around parallel and keep the slide alive. With our flexible equipment, it is a little harder to get our skis broken loose and slipping than it is with rigid Alpine boots and bindings.

Interestingly, once you get used to the parallel slip on cross-country equipment, it gets easier to do, and you come closer to perfecting "pure" parallels. The next exercise should help.

HOCKEY STOPS. I love these. Hockey stops are so much fun that it is worth the work of getting the hill groomed just to learn them. They amaze people who can't do them. And they are so *easy*. Once you get comfortable with hockey stops, you are ready for parallel turns. Basically, it is the same way you stop on ice skates, the same way downhillers stop. Once you know the "trick," it's a snap—and a valuable tool. The hockey stop can get you out of many scrapes. It's really skiing.

To learn, we must start on a nicely packed hill. If you have been hard at this learning process all day, your hill should be right. If this is a new day or if there has been a new snow, let's pack it down a little. About 10 uphills and 10 snowplows down should smooth and pack the snow.

Start downhill in your normal, parallel, knees-bent downhill position. After you have a good bit of speed going, begin to

Hockey Stop. My son Tom is about to plant the pole he'll pivot around. As he passes the planted pole, he levers his ski tails out and stops with a spray of snow.

7.

111

sink down into a slightly deeper crouch. When you are ready to stop, first determine which side you are going to lead with, that is, which ski will end up downhill, doing the most stopping. Frequently, this is your stronger side, the side you are "handed." A right-handed person, then, most often would turn his body to the left in order to lead into the stop with his right ski. Here is another case of a "sweet side." Learn to hockey stop on your stronger side first, and after you understand the principle, practice it on your "off side" until it works both ways.

As soon as you are ready to stop, plant the pole that is opposite your "lead" ski. If you are going to stop with your right ski, plant your left pole in front of you, almost next to your left ski tip, about six inches out from it.

Here's the trick: As you pass your planted pole, unweight* and lever yourself out away from it with an inside flip of your left arm. What you are doing is breaking your skis loose into a side-slip, with tails swinging out faster because you are pushing them out with your left pole.

As you swing down perpendicular to the fall line, "lock everything up." You should generate a satisfying "spray" of snow, with your downhill, leading ski edged slightly into the snow—and you should *stop right away!* Your uphill ski can provide some "stop," too, but its main function is balance. Your downhill pole (the right in this case) does nothing.

When you can hockey stop at will in both directions, you can ski much more ambitious trails. It will allow you to do 90-degree turns at full speed on trails that seemed impossible before. You do not, of course, have to come to a complete stop. You can do a 90-degree turn and "unlock" before you come to a complete stop.

PARALLEL TURNS. Parallel turns are similar to the hockey stop but not as radical. Just as the snowplow stop paved the way for the half-snowplow turn (and, later, the snowplow, or

---

*When we unweight, we simply stand up straight (almost) rapidly and take some of the weight off the skis. Then, it is easier to get them skidding.

beginning stem christie), the hockey stop paves the way for parallel turns, which, in our case, could be called "half-hockey stop" turns. That phrase explains the technique fairly well. If you now understand the transition from snowplow stop to snowplow turn—the fact that the first step is to start your skis slipping sideways—the transition from hockey stop to parallel turn is obvious.

To do parallels, start downhill again on your nice, wide-open hill. Travel right down the fall line, straight downhill. Now we are just going to do a series of half-hockey stops (actually more like quarter-hockey stops). As you go downhill, sink down into a lower crouch. When you are ready to begin your series of parallels, plant the pole that will become the uphill pole, unweight (both with your "jumping up" motion and by using the planted pole for leverage), and start your ski tails slipping

Parallel Turn. First, plant that pole.

114

Parallel Turn (cont.). Next, sink down, unweight, and pivot around the pole. You've just changed directions. This turn works best if done quickly across the fall line.

7.

outward. As soon as they break loose, sink again into the crouch, plant the other pole, unweight, and transfer the side-slip to the other side.

To do parallels correctly, you should weave continuously back and forth across the fall line while attempting to keep your skis skidding sideways, from one side to the other, at all times. Your skis, of course, remain parallel to each other; hence, the term "parallel turns." Linking a series of these turns will control your downhill speed. That is the main purpose of this turn.

When you master the parallel turn, you are ready for ambitious hills. You now can play on those "toboggan hills" that you come across from time to time. The parallel in conjunction with the telemark turn, the final turn we are going to discuss, will enable you to ski downhill in *all* snow conditions, from hard-packed to deep powder. You will be able to ski down hills that are so big that you won't be anxious to turn around and climb straight back up. A seeming paradox, but not really. One of my favorite places affords me a three-quarter mile gentle climb through the woods and a chance to shoot down a hill that is used for motorcycle hill climbing in the summer. The best of both worlds!

Let me throw one big "damper" in here. Nordic skiing is very safe. In this "extra hour" we have partially bridged the gap between Nordic and Alpine skiing. We are actually Alpine skiing (to a limited degree) on cross-country equipment. As the speed goes up, so does the danger. Our equipment still isn't going to break our limbs, but a crash and tumble halfway down a quarter-mile-long, 25-degree hill probably is going to disconnect *something.*

It's fantastic to know how to do all of these maneuvers on cross-country skis, and "pure skiing" will make you a much more competent Nordic skier. But if you find you love the speed and danger of those blasts downhill, you are ready for a couple of

Alpine lessons. You will find that you are already well-schooled in the fundamentals.

THE FAMOUS TELEMARK TURN. About 125 years ago, the telemark was the main turn on those 10-foot long, bent-tipped boards with the leather arch straps. Then stem turns came along, and Nordic and Alpine skiing began to go their separate ways. When Alpine equipment began to get more rigid, the telemark lost favor. Finally, heel tie-downs came along, and the telemark became impossible on Alpine equipment. So it was lost to the downhillers and forgotten.

But it stayed alive in all phases of Nordic skiing. You have seen ski jumpers land in the basic telemark position and end their run-outs with crisp little telemark turns. When Nordic skiing began to emerge from its dark ages in this country, interest in the telemark revived in a big way. *Everybody* wants to learn this maneuver, and rightly so. It is a blast—and it's our most powerful turn.

When we analyze in words what happens during the telemark, the forces involved, it sounds pretty complex. You won't master it in an hour. But I can show it to you and get you to practice, practice, practice. It probably will take you most of a season to get good at the telemark turn.

Telemark Downhill Position. Let's start with the telemark position for downhill. Look at the photograph. It is a deeply knee-bent position. The forward leg (either one) is bent sharply at the knee. The lower portion of the leg is vertical. The trailing leg is far back, with the lower portion of that leg nearly parallel to the back ski. The front foot is flat on its ski, but the trailing foot is sharply bent at the toes. Weight is *evenly* distributed on both feet (awkward at first). Your hands/poles are all over the place in the air, helping you keep your balance on this "tightrope." Your back stays straight up and down, and your eyes are forward and up.

Q. How far back should the trailing ski be?
A. The tip of the trailing ski should be opposite your forward foot.

7.

The Famous Telemark Turn. First, I get in the telemark position, ready to turn downhill. The forward (uphill) knee now begins to drive downhill. The upper body turns in the direction of the turn.

Telemark Turn (cont.). The turn is starting to work. Note that the back ski is steering as much as the front. Now, I'm really leaning into it, with my poles doing their "tightrope" balancing act.

7.

Once you get comfortable with the telemark position, this becomes a tremendously stable way downhill. If you see a mogul (large mound of snow) coming or a bad sitzmark (depression caused by a fallen skier) or a bare spot, go into the telemark. Your front leg is braced, your center of gravity is lowered, and your weight is spread evenly over the longest possible area.

Now, go straight downhill time after time in the telemark position (both right and left legs leading), and as it begins to feel more comfortable, try to switch from "left leading" to "right leading" and vice versa. Make it a clean scissoring. After you do the switch-over a few times, you will begin to feel a little tendency to turn immediately after the switch. You are on your way!

Telemark Turns. In order to turn, simply drive your forward knee in, toward your body, causing the lead ski to stem slightly—and around you come. You always drive the leading knee *in*, so the leading leg determines the direction of the turn: right knee forward, left turn; left knee forward, right turn. Just a few degrees of turn is all you should be getting at this point. More turn will happen as your ability and stability increase.

Incidentally, your upper body turns a little to begin the telemark turn, but it always returns to a normal position over your skis. Your trailing ski is steering, too, and is just about as important as the front ski. As the turn develops, your back leg will pull in under you; as it does, it adds turning power.

Telemark turns swing wider across the fall line than do parallels. Consequently, there is more time between swings, and they look more graceful. You can slow down or speed up your descent by lengthening or shortening your swings, and you actually can come almost to a stop if you want to. You'll feel like a "falling leaf," with all the speed variations.

Tip: Learn and practice the telemark in nice soft snow, four inches deep or more. You probably will fall a lot, and the deeper snow helps the skis "carve" as you go around.

When you have reached the point of linking telemark turns, you have learned all *I* can teach you about cross-country skiing. You are ready for almost anything that comes along. You could go on to racing if you wished to, but racing and touring, even touring with lots of "hill playing," are two different disciplines. You might try a citizen's race to see if you enjoy it. Your kick and glide certainly will get stronger, and that will improve your ability to cover lots of ground effortlessly.

    Well, you are into it now. And you are probably hooked! The trouble, for me, with teaching you through a book is that I don't get to experience *your* enthusiasm as you get turned on. These six or seven hours should have worked some unbelievable magic on you. You no longer complain about winter. Now you can go out and beat it at its own game.
    How did you like the course? I really would like to hear. If you wish to drop me a line, write in care of the publisher. Now let's help each other into our cars, do the last "turn" of the day (the key in the ignition), and go home to the best night's sleep we have had in years.
    Thanks for coming out!

Hour 7.   Timecheck

Take as much time as you want, even the rest of your life if you're having fun.

- ☐ "Helicopter" Turns
- ☐ Snowplow Christies
    - ☐ Right
    - ☐ Left
    - ☐ Linked
- ☐ Hockey Stops
    - ☐ Right
    - ☐ Left
- ☐ Parallel Turns
    - ☐ Right
    - ☐ Left
    - ☐ Linked
- ☐ Telemark Downhill
- ☐ Telemark Turns
    - ☐ Right
    - ☐ Left
    - ☐ Linked

AFTERWORD

✶

Learning to ski the way you just have has deprived you of one of the most satisfying aspects of taking an "adult education" course.

My "live" students seem to enjoy my little bobbles. No, that's not quite right. They *love* to see their instructor crash! Here's your treat for being such good students and doing all the practicing I've asked you to do.

These are the "out-takes" from the action shots in the book.

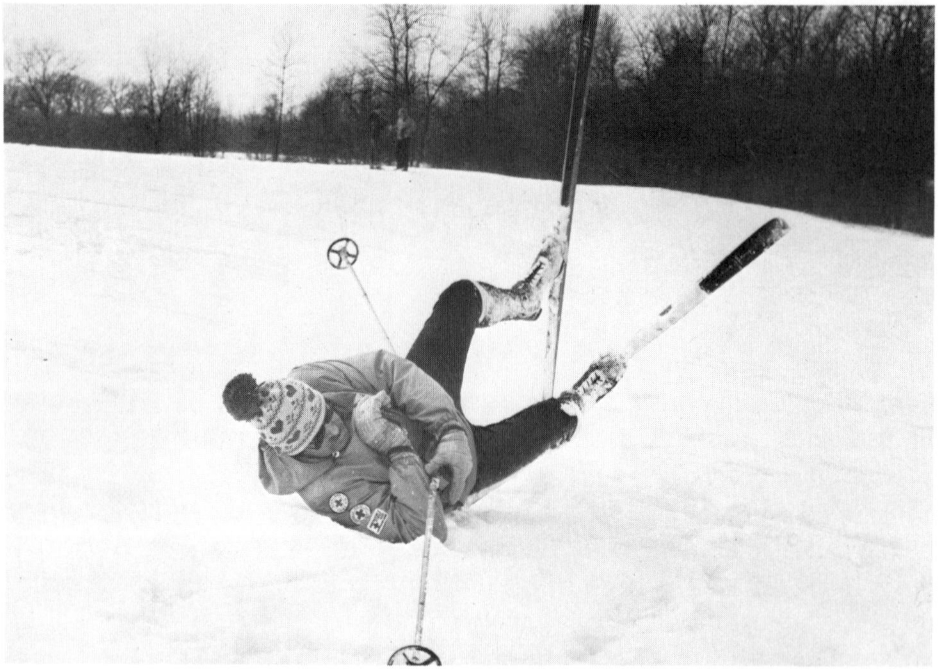

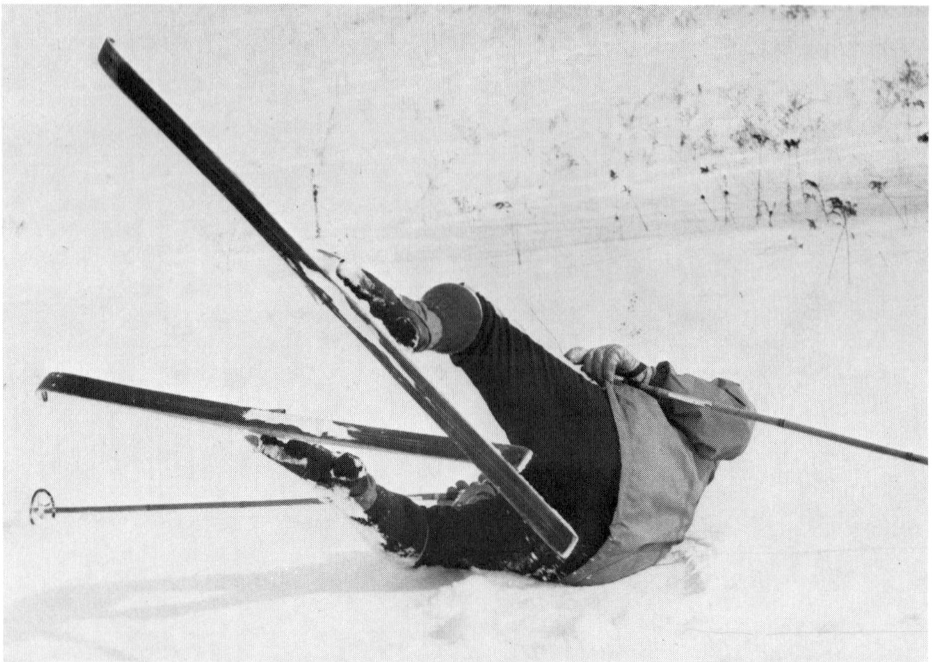